Extra Hands

Grasping for a Meaningful Life

♦♦♦♦♦♦♦

Jack Orchard

To

Drew, Ethan, Claire, Lily, and Poppy

"The most fortunate of us frequently meet with calamities which may greatly afflict us. And to fortify our minds against the attacks of these misfortunes should be one of the principal studies and endeavors of our lives."

♦ Thomas Jefferson

"Never, never, never give up."

♦ Winston Churchill

Chapter One

See for Yourself

◆◆◆◆◆◆◆

If there is a God and you are not a believer, you're screwed. If it turns out that God does not exist and you are a believer, well, then, no harm done. At least, so thought the French philosopher, Blaise Pascal, a prodigious thinker as well as a passionate agnostic for much of his life. Pascal experienced a religious conversion after a near-death experience that involved his horse-drawn carriage nearly plunging over the Neuilly bridge in Paris in 1654, but for those less inclined to mystical visions and more inclined to game theory, the former mathematician drafted his now famous conversion wager.

I am on my deathbed now, and the same age as Pascal was when he died at age thirty-nine. Unlike him, I feel no conversion coming. No bright lights, no Biblical voices. Just the ordinary sights and sounds of St. Louis, Missouri, where I have chosen to live my last days. Yet, like Pascal, as I approach death I can now reflect on the memorable moments and lessons learned that have informed my way.

Rather than the hands of God, I feel symptoms, each one ominous and banal, each one unannounced and unbidden. They came by slow degrees. So subtle were they that it's difficult to pinpoint exactly when

1

they began, but I know that in 2000, around the time of my wedding, I felt a weakness in my left hand.

My wife, Eve, and I had plenty of money, active lives, and a three-story home in San Francisco's Richmond district, a house that opened onto a small but immaculately manicured park known as Mountain Lake Park. We had just moved there from a loft in downtown San Francisco surrounded by glass skyscrapers and 24-hour traffic, so the bucolic setting represented our lush green future. Birds chattered, dogs barked, the sun battled the fog each morning, and every time I gripped something with my left hand, whether a golf club, a door knob, or a hand towel, I could feel something was not quite right. The joint in my thumb would not bend tightly with my fingers, as if it were participating with my fingers while gripping something, but doing so reluctantly. By the late summer, around the time of my 33rd birthday, my legs began to feel strange as well, unusually stiff any time I became chilled.

Every day Eve would come home from work, toss her purse on the breakfast table and rummage around in the fridge for something tasty for dinner. I would emerge from my home office on the top floor and gingerly walk down the creaky stairs while clinging to the banister with both hands. "Jack, is that you?" she'd call.

I'd come in the kitchen, watching my hands as I opened and closed my fists. I could smell onions frying in olive oil, lemons, and fresh parsley. Because I wanted to think about opening a bottle of Chardonnay, not about fighting with the corkscrew, and because I wanted only to pour the wine into our wedding gift glasses and toast our new life in this place we had always wanted, I answered, "It's me." Though in truth, I was no longer sure.

I had always been robustly healthy, and now I couldn't depend on my hands to open a bottle of wine. Who am I if I can no longer do what I have always done? If I can't tie my shoes anymore either, does that make me less who I once was? And how do others see me? Do they think my mind is no more capable than my body? These days, seven years later, my symptoms having progressed to where I can no longer walk, can no longer get out of a chair, or talk, or type, life has become an act of faith, a faith that is tactile, physical, and visible in every attempt I make. My arms, my legs, my tongue, my breath – these are no longer mine to command. What were once simple tasks are now impossibilities. Gravity has defeated me.

Although we are not surprised when a spiritual person turns towards spirituality in a personal crisis, we wonder how others cope when faced with tragedy. What do they believe in, and how does it comfort them? My deepest faith is in curiosity. Illness has stolen my strength and withered my body to skin and bones, but for me the sustaining, ineradicable shape is the question mark, a piece of punctuation that opens every ending.

My earliest questions as a young boy were probably at once mundane and transcendent, a style typical of toddlers. Why are trees green? How long is a day on Pluto? Why do I have to eat my vegetables? I asked kid questions from morning to night, quirky and silly and real questions that my parents did their best to take seriously and answer.

When I was sixteen an archeologist friend of my parents came to dinner, and as I listened to him describe his latest project in Greece I realized just how many questions a person can ask and how far they can lead. Professor Sarantis Symeonoglou told us how he had wandered recently on a hillside on the island of Ithaca where he found a pottery shard sticking out of an eroded embankment lining the dusty road that snaked over the hill. Because his eyes were expertly trained to hypothesize a whole from its parts, he recognized the design painted on the shard as something from the 12th century B.C., when the fabled warrior Odysseus supposedly lived there. He told us how he had petitioned the Greek government for a license to search for Odysseus' palace, and after much preparatory work and fundraising, had received the first such license issued since the mid-1920s. He named the dig the Odyssey Project, and scheduled excavation to begin the following summer. And then my parents asked me a question: Would I like to go to Ithaca on the dig?

My parents had always pushed me and my siblings to explore. I had trekked across Alpine glaciers, biked from town to town in the Dutch countryside, and walked the lake country of northern Wales. But every time I was with a group of other students and a pair of guides who spoke the language. Not so now.

I attended Professor Symeonoglou's seminar at Washington University to learn the basics of archeology and meet the others on the dig team. They traveled to Ithaca all together in late May 1984 while I

4

stayed behind to finish school. Then, the day after my last exam I waved goodbye to my parents and set out on my own. The dig director had given me a page of instructions to follow, in English for me and in Greek for anyone I might need to ask for help, my own Rosetta Stone. 'Fly to Athens and stay at the such-and-such hotel. In the morning take the bus to Patras, then board the ferry to Ithaca, and we'll meet you at the dock.'

I found the hotel without a problem, but over-slept the next morning. When I awoke and realized how little time I had to get to the bus station I darted around the room in a cold sweat stuffing my belong-ings back in my suitcase. I flew out into the hallway and down the staircase, and jumped in a taxi. As the driver pulled into the bus station he saw my bus pull-ing out and jumped out to stop it for me. I gave him a big tip and then climbed aboard the bus, sweaty and shaken, gave the driver my ticket, and sat with my head in my hands. I was alone in a place where I knew neither the language, nor the land. Even the signs, all in Greek letters, were indecipherable. The only thing familiar was the sight of the Acropolis towering over the city, white and majestic. The rest didn't look like the Athens I knew from school texts, the ancient city where Socrates had given up his life rather than for-sake his commitment to critical reason. At least it didn't look that way on the surface.

On the ferry from Patras the day I arrived, the island of Ithaca looked imposing. I saw a land mass, small but mountainous, its terrain rising steeply from the Ionian Sea. I had expected to find an exotic Greek paradise with white villas spread over its hillsides. Instead, the Ithaca I found had eastern and northern faces green with scrub, currant vines, and olive groves; its southern and western faces were generally dusty brown under the dry, hot sun of the eastern Mediterranean. The ferry approached from the east, and then turned south and east to enter the protected pocket bay of Vathi, Ithaca's largest town with a population of about 2,000. When the ferry pulled into port, I stood near the door to the gangway. It was the weekend of national elections. Although I didn't know it at the time, behind me stood the local representative to the Greek parliament. When I stepped from the ferry, hundreds of people began to wave and cheer, and I thought, "Yes, I'm amazed I made it this far too."

On the island, all the members of the dig team managed the various activities – site planning, trench excavation, artifact identification, artifact cleaning, artifact reconstruction, photography, and surveying. Local laborers did the actual digging. I worked with the dig's surveyor most of the time. We plotted the entire dig area one square meter at a time, several acres in all, using a surveyor's distance measure, a level, and a range pole.

Each day after leaving the site we would haul our cache of antiquities down into Vathi to the island's museum. A lonely and quiet building with Ionic columns and a classical cornice, the museum sat at the far eastern end of Vathi's bay. The exterior could have used a new paint job, and the interior needed even more help. I wondered why it seemed so neglected until about a week into the dig when I realized that when you live in a place of such historical significance it's almost absurd to build a structure to showcase its many wonders. Our pottery washing crew was probably the most action that museum had seen in decades. We sorted every man-made object we pulled from the trenches, and gently washed away the dirt. While ancient roof tiles made up much of our haul, we also found countless shards of clay pots of every size and description, some with beautiful decorations.

I photographed every artifact we unearthed. In the viewfinder I saw pottery pieces shaped like diamonds, icicle-shaped shards, two-inch painted surfaces. I clicked my shutter and in my mind's eye I saw a woman bending over a cooking vessel, a child lugging a water carrier, a man holding a ceremonial staff. That was when I first understood the power of deducing a whole from its parts, imagining backwards from an effect to its cause. We hypothesized and reconstructed an entire village, an entire life – domestic life, worship practices, funereal rites – from the most infinitesimal clues.

One of the assistant dig directors, Marylou, was the team fecalologist. Each morning after a quick breakfast of yogurt, ginger rolls, and instant coffee Professor Symeonoglou would say, "Marylou, get your shit together! Let's go everyone." One day, on the drive up to the dig site, Marylou explained that from a 3,000 year-old fecal sample you can deduce much about the diet, and hence the lifestyle, of the person who produced it. How heavily did he depend on hunting meat to eat? Did she survive on fruits and vegetables? What kind of agriculture might he have practiced?

Digging is a kind of question. We discover answers that we record and from which we hypothesize, and then we subject our conclusions to public scrutiny. We adhere to scientific method, that is, we seek a "reliable, consistent, and non-arbitrary" representation of our observable world. We value a truth that's free of bias and prejudice. We put our minds to a rational explanation and we cling to it until we can construct another one that better explains our observations, at which time we abandon the old one like a leaky rowboat.

On the one hand, what I found that summer under Marylou's tutelage was a centuries-old pile of poop, but when looked at under a magnifying lens, it was also a civilization waiting to tell its story. The lessons of Socrates were there, not in the soil or the artifacts we unearthed, but in our process of finding, examining, questioning, trying to explain everything we found, and just as importantly, what we did not find.

My story too was just beginning. Then – a shock of bright red hair on my head, my forearms freckled and tanned by the sun – I dove into a subterranean world no modern person had ever seen, and a way of thinking developed millennia ago by someone who valued truth above all, truth in the world around him and truth in his own life.

In some ways, at this point in my life, I am that boy again, in a strange and sometimes frightening place. Twenty-three years after my summer on Ithaca,

I am once again unable to communicate, dependent on others, and facing the greatest unknown. I have learned navigational strategies and grown more confident and resourceful. I have recovered from mishaps in foreign countries and improvised solutions. And now. irretrievably stuck in the greatest challenge of my life, that training and experience are the only tools I have left, and the only tools I need.

If you treat someone like a kid, the odds are he will act like one. But if you reinforce a sixteen year-old's emerging self-image as an independent-thinking and acting adult, you will likely get just that. That summer in Ithaca, although I was the youngest member of the team by a decade, the others expected me to work as hard as they did, to invest myself completely in the dig.

Most nights we ate dinner at a small restaurant in Vathi's main drag which wrapped around the southeast corner of the bay along the water. We were exhilarated to smell the same sea as Homer once had, but at the end of the day we were also tired, dusty, and most of all – thirsty. One of my new friends asked the waitress for a round of beers; to supplement his meager Greek, he gestured to show the upending of a glass, laughed, and then waved his hand over the rest of us seated at the table. The waitress laughed too, smiled at us hulking Americans, and wrote something down on her pad. A few minutes later, she appeared with a tray of ice-cold beers in large, frosty mugs. As she set them on the table one by one she smiled and taught us how to say large beer in Greek, *megalo mpira.* She passed the mugs around to everyone at the table, including me. I had worked alongside these people all day and it stood to reason I could drink alongside them at night. I tipped my head back and gulped the beer as if it were nothing unusual. The bitter local brew burned my throat at first, but it made me feel as if I, too, was an adult. We ate moussaka and fresh calamari, big white blocks of fresh feta cheese with fat tomatoes, and tangy black olives like they were candy. Someone ordered another round of beers, and again included me in the count. I was ecstatic.

Everything about that summer was magical. I was thrilled by the thought that if we found evidence of Odysseus' palace underground we would rewrite history. All the textbooks would have to be changed. We had begun digging at a spot described by Homer himself, and marked by the summer solstice, which made me feel like every dirt clod could contain a piece of ancient wisdom. It made me wonder what the world might look like today if the great library at Alexandria had not burned, if dogma had not overpowered reason to usher in the Dark Ages, if more of that wisdom had survived.

One Sunday that summer we went to the beach at Filiatra, a few miles northeast of Vathi. We had been invited by the mayor of Vathi who enjoyed hobnobbing with foreign visitors to Ithaca. I hadn't been sure I wanted to go, but immediately agreed to go when I heard that one of the beach-goers would be Amanda, who besides being a graduate student in archeology at Washington University, and one of the dig's assistant directors, was jaw-droppingly gorgeous.

The beach was small, no more than half a mile long, and covered in small pebbles. It wraps around a small, secluded bay that is relatively shallow, only fifty feet deep at its deepest point before opening into the sea. While much of the Mediterranean is an azure blue, the water at Filiatra was shallow enough to be shockingly clear. I waded into the water and swam out to the middle of the bay. Without goggles, I couldn't make out the details on the floor of the bay, but the water was so clear that when I put my head under the surface I felt as if I were floating in mid-air.

Back on the beach, I saw the mayor throwing a live squid he had caught repeatedly against a rock; tenderizing the meat, I guessed. Amanda was chatting with him and laughing into her cupped hands, her hair bright as sunlight and her long, tanned legs stretched out on her beach towel. I tried not to stare at this real life enactment of my dream life. And then, as if she had felt my gaze, Amanda shouted over my way, "How's the water, Jack?"

"Great," I said, a stupid grin on my face.

As a kid, I had devoured the Greek myths. I rooted for Hercules as he performed his twelve labors, sympathized with Prometheus chained to a rock, and wanted to tell Sisyphus to give it a rest. But they were just stories with colorful characters. Surely, no one believes in a group of deities sitting on top of Mount Olympus anymore, right? But then how do we decide where fiction ends and faith begins?

My parents sent my siblings and me to religious school on Sunday mornings at a Reform Jewish temple in suburban St. Louis, not so much to embrace the rituals of Judaism, but to learn about our heritage, understand our history, and explore our conception of morality to determine what we value and why.

Rabbi Rosenbloom was a small, slim man. Nearly bald on the top of his head, he grew his hair long in back. His closely set eyes, long nose, and easy smile gave him an approachable presence, and his reading spectacles, low on his nose, made him look as erudite as he actually was. On Sundays, we would study in classrooms for about two hours, and afterwards move to the synagogue for a short service and sermon. Rabbi Rosenbloom led the students in recitations of various traditional blessings in Hebrew and English, then read from an ornate Torah before delivering a sermon. He spoke with little formality, and approached his topics intellectually, grounded in reason and humanitarian ethics over the teachings of the Torah or Talmud. Judaism was and still is for me a cultural identity, a connection to a collective history, and a set of values.

In Ithaca, that summer, I thought about the muses Homer invoked at the beginning of the Odyssey, and the Greek myths of my boyhood. It all seemed a part of my youth, saturated as it was with questions as numerous as ripples on the Ionian Sea all around us. Standing on an island hilltop, a kind of faith burgeoned in me, one anchored in discovery, openness, and hope. Erich Fromm's definition of hope made sense to me then and makes sense to me now; "To be ready at every moment for that which is not yet born, and yet not become desperate if there is no birth in our lifetime." In other words, I learned to hold two opposing ideas at one time – to expect everything and accept nothing. This kind of faith taught me I could conquer my fear of the unknown by plunging head first into what frightened me. As I did then, at sixteen, alone on an ancient island, I do now, when every day I am closer to my final shore.

During the excavation of one of the first trenches on Ithaca, the local day laborers we hired to do the actual digging swung their pick-axes wild and free. The dry, rocky soil crumbled around them, and as they dug the trench became littered with pottery shards, many painted with people or animals. Pick, pick, pick went the steady rhythm of their axes. Suddenly, we all heard a loud crunch. The trench manager jumped into the hole, reached down, and gathered a handful of fragments to show to Professor Symeonoglou. He examined them carefully, ran his fingers over the edges, scraped dirt off the painted decorations. There were the remains of a small vase that had lay buried under the earth for thousands of years, undisturbed, and judging from the clean edges of the shards, intact.

Before it was smashed, the six-inch vase with a narrow body, small foot, and delicate handle had probably been a tear vase, once used to collect the waters of a good cry. Who had used this delicate vessel? Maybe it was Penelope herself, the loyal wife of Odysseus. The goddess Athena would occasionally visit Penelope in her dreams to spare her from nights otherwise spent weeping for her lost hero. No, the decorations on the vase indicated it was made during the classical period, around 800 B.C., rather than the end of the Mycenaean period, circa 1200 B.C., when Odysseus was said to have lived. Perhaps the tear vase was used by someone who listened as a bard sang Homer's verses about the reunion of Odysseus and his dutiful son Telemachus after they had spent twenty years apart.

Although I could not have known it at the time, the tear vase now seems a symbol of the future awaiting me. Before it was discovered it was pristine and beautiful, but in being revealed it lost its beauty, although not its significance. For no matter how whole the vase remained, it could never have held a fraction of human sadness, neither Penelope's aching loneliness nor my frightening descent into paralysis. When I think now about those shards lying in the ditch, I think the vase represents the frailty of human life, the broken promise of longevity, and the tender beauty of each mundane moment in our short lives. But most of all, the vase speaks to me about the enduring nature of discovery. If you dig down and find a beautiful thing, it does not, in the end, matter if it is whole or in pieces, because it is there, in the dirt, hurt and human.

Chapter Two

Be Prepared

◆◆◆◆◆◆◆

I was born in Saint Louis, Missouri, on August 11th, 1967, to Robert and Lois Orchard. My Dad was forty-six, my Mom twenty-nine, an age differential I thought little about as a child. When I was very young, a baby, a boy, my parents seemed static to me, two icons frozen in role, in time, their singular purpose to raise me and my siblings. Biologically, I'm the third of my Mom's four children, and the first of my Dad's two, although none of us uses the term 'half-brother' or 'half-sister' because my Dad is the only father any of us has ever known or wanted to know.

My sister, Connie, is the oldest, six years older than I am. When we were kids she was always a stage ahead of me, graduating from high school when I was graduating from elementary school, out of college by the time I was starting it, so although we always got along, we also had little common ground on which to be especially close. Next is my brother, Jay, four years older than I am. His learning challenges, and the struggle he endured as he came to understand them, made it difficult for me, for anyone really, to relate to him, but inside he has a gentle, generous, and caring heart. Then there's Harry, two years younger than I am, the youngest of the family. Before I left for college we were inseparable, the very best of friends, and though we did not live in the same city for the next thirteen years, we remained just as close.

Some peoples' memories of their childhood are crisp, as though the brain is an airtight tin that stores pictures of the past, an occasional video, but my memories are hazy, filled with fog. I remember certain smells, an Impressionist drawing of two brothers we had hanging on the dining room wall, and my fifth birthday, occurring in the high heat of summer, the bushes in the backyard a dozen shades of green thanks to my Mom's even greener thumb. I recall the furniture in my parents' bedroom, its particular positioning, the simple black headboard topped with dozens of books, and the ottoman at the foot of the bed, onto which my Mom pulled me, hugged me hard and close.

"Jack," she said, "you're growing up, getting big now," and then she said, "That means we need you to help around the house. You can start by setting the dinner table each night, and picking up your clothes." To a teenager such a remark might have been greeted with resentment but to a small boy it conferred a sense of significance. My Mom gave me the feeling that what I did could impact the people around me.

I thought often about that, especially when hiding in a dark cubbyhole in my Dad's study, my favorite daydreaming locale. Between a built-in sofa and the wall to one side of it there was a space about three feet wide, tall, and deep. The top of the hole was part of the sofa's armrest that extended out to form a sort of side table. My Dad kept nothing in the hole but a small waste basket, so it was a perfect place in which a small boy could disappear. As I sat there in the dark I imagined fantastic scenarios – Jack the conqueror of monsters, Jack the king of the world. In my secret place, hidden from anyone and everyone, I also imagined I had never been born, and wondered what my family might have been like without me. Existing isn't enough, my Mom had said. If you want to matter to other people you have to do something. Sitting quietly in a hole you don't affect the people around you, and you could choose to live your whole life in such solitude. But there's so much joy to experience outside that hole, learning and growing.

At the neighborhood public school, with my chin resting on my hands and my gaze fixed at some point above the blackboard, my thoughts regularly drifted away from multiplication tables and geography to the world beyond the school's front doors. As my parents took me along when they ran errands I noticed that some people spoke very quickly, as if they harbored a deep secret about words that compelled them to spit them out as fast as their tongues could manage. Others spoke with a numbing slowness, as if they knew the same secret as the fast-talkers but interpreted what to do about it differently. What had they discovered that I didn't yet know? There must be a limit, I thought. When you've spoken your predetermined number of words you're finished speaking for the rest of your life. Fast-talkers must not have the willpower to resist the temptation to find their limit. They jabber on with no regard for their future silence. Slow-talkers are cautious and prudent. They choose their words carefully and speak as few as possible to make themselves understood.

Connie was the fast-talker in the family, and Harry wasn't much slower. One day they'll regret it, I thought. At least they'll have my Dad to help them, not a slow-talker compared to some people I had heard, but a judicious conversationalist. He didn't waste words at all, but spoke exactly those he needed and let their meaning float in the air above the dining room table for the rest of us to digest. The smart choice is obvious, I thought – make your point and shut up. I resolved to speak carefully always.

Yet now I am mute as a statue. My illness stole my voice, first its timbre, then its volume, and eventually its last squeaky whisper. My childhood fantasy proved much more real than fantastic. But I had been careful, so careful, ever since then. How could I have hit my limit while still in my thirties?

If you aren't going to talk much, and your Mom won't let you watch TV, there isn't much else to do after sundown but read. I sat by my Dad most nights picking out the letters j, a, c, and k in his newspaper as he skimmed through the headlines. As a result, I learned to read before first grade, an accomplishment that did more to ensure my boredom than my intellect, at least at that point in my life. During math class, my knack for numbers emerged, and when I wasn't fiddling with $+$ and $\%$ and $<$ and $>$ I was in the traveling library mobile. My parents noticed that I generally chose books that explain how things work, like rain clouds, or fire engines. They gave me some books by David Macaulay, the author and illustrator of books about how things are built and how they work. I pored through each of them – Castle, Cathedral, Underground, and Pyramid – until the pages became smudged and dog-eared. Especially in Underground, Macaulay reveals the vast and beautiful infrastructure beneath city streets. I learned to appreciate the idea that just because you don't know how something works doesn't mean it can't be explained. Investigation reveals. I would start digging for answers and before long I'd end up in China.

My third grade teacher noticed that I wasn't paying attention in class, and told my Mom that maybe I should go to a different school with smaller classes where teachers could devote more attention to trying to engage me. The next year they sent me to a small, private school where I met Mrs. Witscher.

Hers was the very first class I attended as a new student in September of 1976. I remember entering her classroom, sitting down quietly, hoping not to be noticed. We were all summer-baked boys and girls, still carrying with us our tans and sandals. Most teachers, at the start of a new school year, say something like "nice to see you, hello, how was your vacation," but not Mrs. Witscher. She stood in front of the class and without a word of introduction said, "Open your books to page 18. Copy the problem onto a blank sheet of paper."

Wait a minute. I didn't have any paper. I didn't even have a pencil. At my old school, we worked on blackboards, needed only chalk. Now, I sat there scared, at sea, feeling my conundrum with the intensity only a child can, as though I were without food on a raft in the Atlantic.

All around me the other kids, prepped for prep school by years of prior experience, were scribbling away. I raised my hand.

"Yes, Mr. Orchard," she said.

My name. She knew my name. How could this be? We had never even met. The fact that she knew my name only added to my trepidation, and, oddly, did not make me feel so much visible as transparent, seen through, defenseless.

"I don't have paper or a pencil," I mumbled.

I have no memory of the sounds in the room but I can still see Mrs. Witscher's eyes open wide, like two bear traps ready to snap shut on my shaking legs. The chalk in her hand dropped from her fingers to the floor, shattering into pieces. Then she said the words I have never forgotten, words that carried me on to high school, to the drafty lecture halls at Harvard, then to the wood paneled offices on Wall Street, the dingy alleys of Moscow, and to here, where I am now, in my study with a ventilator pushing air into my lungs through a tube inserted in my throat. My hair stood on end as she opened her mouth to speak.

"Mr. Orchard," she said. "There is no substitute for preparedness."

No, there most certainly is not. Despite my anxiety and self-consciousness then I understood her completely. It was a code by which to live my life. In this sense, Mrs. Witscher was my Maimonedes. But her comment also led to false hope, because it implies that preparedness is always possible. Her comment, or my interpretation of it, rested on the naïve faith that foresight and control are attainable. Often they are. But just as often they are not, and the best education teaches this – not only how to succeed by anticipating the challenges we may face, and then preparing to meet those challenges, but also how to react when our predictions are wrong, when our preparation is inadequate and we fail utterly. We all have to leave childhood behind, and this involves taking responsibility for our failures and hopefully learning not to repeat them.

That school, and the high school I attended, left little room for failure. They were nurturing institutions where teachers paid attention to each student and quickly reported every academic misstep to parents. I was a good student, so I didn't suffer the agony of failure until later. In fact, I loved going to school, and didn't miss a single day from seventh through twelfth grade. I played football every Fall which was a fantastic rush, smashing full-speed into my friends dressed in our armor, although I got the wind knocked out of me the first time someone hit me. I also joined the school musical in tenth to twelfth grades, partly because I enjoyed singing, but even more because I enjoyed dancing onstage with the girls. Educationally my strong suit was math thanks to Eric Hanson.

Mr. Hanson always used two chalkboards, which were hung close together on the west and north walls of his classroom, so he could write equations and proofs that bled over from one to the other. He was tall and red-haired, like me, and he had a salt-and-cayenne beard that made him look professorial. The elegance of a good proof would make his voice rise.

Moving with his equations, he'd leap across from one board to the other to show the flow of the problem. If he couldn't leap far enough to land his finger on the answer to a question like, "And where do we find the derivative of this function?!" he would just sling his chalk at the answer because that was the fastest way to get there. His energy was infectious. It was impossible not to love whatever he taught.

In November 1984 I was in Mr. Hanson's calculus class when my life changed, although I didn't know it, and was entirely unprepared for it. My Dad had been at work when he felt pressure in his chest and a dull ache in his left arm. He recognized the warning signs of a heart attack, and quickly called his secretary in to drive him to the hospital. Calling an ambulance was not an option in his mind because he was the head of a privately owned corporation. If the employees got spooked it could have damaged the company's operations, so my Dad and his secretary walked calmly out of the building. He called my Mom shortly after he arrived at the hospital, but they didn't tell my siblings and me until Harry and I came home from school. It was just before Thanksgiving so Connie had flown in for the holiday from San Francisco, where she was living, and Jay was home from college.

We all met at the hospital and were briefed by his doctor about his condition. I don't remember the details of what caused the heart attack, or what they did to treat him, but its implications sank in when the doctor said the average survival time for someone his age, then sixty-four, was ten years. When they waited hours to tell me what had happened it upset me that they didn't consider me mature enough to handle bad news. Wasn't I the same person who had just proven himself among a team of professionals on Ithaca? I wasn't a boy anymore. Then, when the doctor said my Dad would likely die in the next ten years, I sped past upset straight to devastated.

I had spent a great part of my life trying to prove myself to him. To me he was a giant. If he would be at the brink of death with every heartbeat going forward, then the primary motivation of my life would be in constant jeopardy. Before that day I thought I needed many years, and that I had plenty of time.

Fortunately, the attack he suffered had been minor. By getting to the hospital quickly, and remaining relaxed from the first warning signs all the way to the emergency room, he had minimized the permanent damage to his heart. They kept him for a week to run more tests. In the cardiac intensive care unit the doctor ordered him kept on a ventilator to ensure that he would not lose oxygen in case of another heart attack. The tubes running in his mouth and down into his windpipe made it impossible for him to speak, but as I stood by his bedside he grabbed my hand and started squeezing out messages in Morse code just like he had done in the navy during World War II. I called the nurse to give me a Morse cheat-sheet. His first message was "need crushed ice."

The next several years were difficult for me. Although my Dad swallowed forty-six pills a day and his doctors were pleased with his condition, I still wondered every time I boarded a plane for Boston if the view of him waving goodbye at the jetway would be the last time I would see him alive. I had recurring nightmares which played out his death in every imaginable circumstance, as if my mind were running through possible scenarios to prepare itself for the jolt when one would come true. I started carrying a Morse code cheat-sheet in my wallet so I would be ready for the next attack. There is no substitute for preparedness.

Six years later, my fears of his imminent demise having been dulled by countless departures from St. Louis, we decided to go on a vacation together to St. Barth's in the Caribbean. At the time, I was working in New York at Merrill Lynch on a team that financed utilities in the south. As the low man on the totem pole, I put in so many hours at the office I might as well have given up my apartment and just established legal residence in my cubicle. On St. Barth's, my Dad and I spent a week soaking up the sun in paradise. I went windsurfing while he lounged by the resort's pool wearing nothing but a pair of thirty-year old sunglasses and a smile. He is a consummate charmer, and made sure to say hello to every skinny, topless girl that walked by. Unfortunately, the color he was turning in the hot island sun masked his graying pallor underneath. His medications had caused an ulcer, and his blood thinners made sure it couldn't heal. I didn't see a thing, and he probably didn't feel blanched while we were there. But when he landed back in St. Louis where my Mom met him at the airport, his face had turned distinctly gray. They drove straight to the hospital.

With his abdomen bleeding internally his heart had to work harder and harder with less and less blood moving through it. Not long after they arrived the vicious cycle broke. He had another heart attack. Because of the ulcer, the doctors had few options. They could give him more blood but they couldn't thin it further. They could try to stop the internal bleeding but it could place so much stress on the heart that he might have another attack, a severe and fatal one.

I had flown back to New York via San Juan where we parted ways. I landed and went straight to work. In my cubicle the phone rang minutes after I settled in with a fresh cup of coffee. My Mom gave me a brief update. I raced back to the airport, caught the next available flight to St. Louis, and met everyone at the hospital. When I arrived he was in the middle of another attack.

We stood outside the ICU dumbstruck and crying. After an hour his condition was stable enough that I could go in for a few seconds but they warned me to get out quickly. I approached his bedside, and was shocked by the tangle of tubes sticking out of him and the cacophony of beeping monitors all around him. He was lying flat, his eyes closed, his belly rising in time with the ventilator shoved in his mouth. I put a hand on his left arm. His eyes opened and he smiled as best he could when I told him I was home. I said I loved him. Then my time was up. A nurse shooed me away like a pigeon.

I spent a sleepless night at home, and arrived at the hospital the next morning as he was going into surgery for a quadruple bypass operation. The waiting was excruciating. I was too anxious to read the book I had brought with me, so I just sat staring at the clock. Finally the surgeon emerged to announce that the operation had been successful. We listened carefully as he explained the procedure in a strangely detached tone, like a car mechanic would do. "When we opened up the hood we found the fuel lines were more clogged than we thought after the diagnostic. So I installed some new lines and patched up that hole in the fuel tank. You should get another 10,000 miles out of him. Make sure he avoids leaded gas." Then he turned and addressed me directly. "The same goes for you, kid. You're the same make and model."

I had never before thought seriously about my health. I had no allergies, no difficulty with my weight, not even a single broken bone. The most serious problem I had faced was the "kissing disease," mononucleosis, while in college. But the surgeon was right. My Dad's heart disease ran in the family. His father, Herman Orchard, died of a heart attack on the operating table in 1952 at the age of sixty-one. He basically scared himself to death during a minor procedure. And Herman's father, Leopold Orchard, also died of a heart attack, in 1927 at age seventy-six. So when the surgeon warned me about "leaded gas," high-cholesterol foods, I took him seriously. I adjusted my diet – less beef, more chicken and fish; less eggs and dairy products, more veggies and fruits.

Since the onset of my illness I've thought often about those episodes at the hospital, especially when I've been hospitalized myself. When I began having difficulty chewing and swallowing I had a feeding tube placed through my abdominal wall into my stomach. Although it didn't require being sedated, the surgeon needed to run a thin catheter with a tiny camera on its tip up my nose and then down through my esophagus into my stomach to choose the best place for the incision. It set off terrible gagging and coughing which made it very difficult to breathe. As I lay on the operating table I thought of my Dad's serenity during his heart attacks, his calm focus on survival which probably saved his life. And I remembered the story he had told me about his father's perilous opposite approach. Short of breath and shivering from the cool air in the operating room, I tried to regain a rhythmic breathing pattern and ignore the tickling catheter shoved in me. By the time I had found a measure of peace the surgeon had finished. And I was still alive.

My apartment building in New York had a small gym in it with a pair of treadmills. I didn't have any free time to use the gym during my first year in New York, but in my second, there was a new person at the bottom of the office hierarchy. So I started running in the mornings before work, three miles at first. It took a half-hour when I began, but I picked up the pace a little more each day. One weekend I bought a heart rate monitor at a running store in my neighborhood. The instructions said that 220 minus your age is roughly your maximum heart rate, and that maintaining a heart rate around 80% of the maximum for a half hour each day would constitute an effective aerobic regimen. I targeted a heart rate of 165, and before long I could get in about six miles in forty-five minutes.

There is something special about a ticking clock, or a looming deadline. No matter what you're doing, you push yourself harder when there's a countdown. My Dad's seemingly precarious health ticked in the back of my mind every day after that first visit to the emergency room in 1984. I wanted to earn his pride like any father's son, and although I never doubted I had it, I've always felt driven to press further and climb higher because of it, to be prepared each day to lose him knowing I did all I could to be worthy of his name. Now, in the twilight of my abbreviated life, I have no regrets about days wasted because I have wasted so few.

Chapter Three

Adapt or Perish

◆◆◆◆◆◆◆

A secret team of scientists in Moscow has made an astonishing breakthrough by inventing the world's largest microchip. Retold often by locals, the joke plays on the Russian predilection for all things big. A quick tour of Moscow will confirm the origins of the joke – the fourteen-lane avenues that encircle the ancient capital, the immense squares over which so many tanks and missile carriers once trundled, and the tremendous Stalinist Gothic skyscrapers built within eyesight of every Moscow vantage point save the subway. All conspire to impress upon the average pedestrian a feeling of personal smallness that is unequaled in most places in the world with the exception of perhaps New York City.

I first visited Moscow in August 1991, just three days before a group of eight "hard-line" members of the Communist Party attempted a coup d'etat to overthrow Mikhail Gorbachev. They blamed him for the Soviet Union's creeping loss of superpower status, its diminution from a nation large, powerful, and intimidating to one shriveled and sickly. By 1991, after two decades of slow deterioration and six years of rapid infrastructural rot, the Soviet Union was thoroughly broken. Grandiose buildings that once housed tsars suffered the indignity of pocked walls. Children begged in the streets, tugging at the pants of business-men waiting in line for a Big Mac in the McDonald's in Pushkin Square. Elderly pensioners hawked salami or an old pair of boots for a few rubles in front of the Bolshoi Theater. Skinny, teenage prostitutes trolled the sidewalks throughout the city-center. The once-colorful buildings sagged under gray skies, dilapidated and somber.

Much of the developed world hailed the collapse of Communism as the revolution of our time, an opportunity to stabilize international relations after the end of the Cold War. But Russia still had a tremendous arsenal of nuclear weapons which, if allowed to come under the control of another totalitarian or nationalistic regime, could make the world much less stable. To seize the opportunity, the U.S. and the nations of Western Europe felt they had to assist those of Eastern Europe and the former Soviet Union as they changed over to market-based economies, believing that economic prosperity would promote peace.

In college I had studied developmental economics, a field that attempts to explain the economic forces at work in nations during major transformations, so I was eager to join the revolution and enact the theories of my college textbooks. I left my job on Wall Street and moved to London to join a new bank focused on financing new ventures in the East. I was twenty-four when I started working there, and I didn't know how to analyze a company's operations, read its balance sheet, or scrutinize its management. But my boss didn't mind. "You'll adapt," he said.

On that first trip to Moscow I went to visit a new phone company, one of the first private corporations to be established there since before the October Revolution in 1917, and came away awestruck by the enormous potential. After seventy-five years of having been deprived of a rising standard of living, the 150 million people in Russia wanted everything the West had to offer, from blue jeans to Mercedes and everything in between. We invested as fast as we could. For a guy pining for action and adventure, Moscow could not be topped.

In addition to learning corporate finance, there was another lesson waiting for me in Russia, a crash course in individual liberties. Having grown up where, as it is written in the Declaration of Independence, "governments are instituted among men, deriving their just powers from the consent of the governed; that whenever any form of government becomes destructive of these ends, it is the right of the people to alter or to abolish it," I was fascinated to explore a culture where autocracy had prevailed for more than a thousand years.

In the early 1700s, Peter the Great conscripted serfs from all across his empire to build him a new capital in the swamps of what became St. Petersburg. Tens of thousands of them perished, either marching there under armed guard, or during construction. Joseph Stalin's victims are so numerous and varied that historians can't agree on which of them to count. Those whom he executed or repressed to death number about 4 million. And yet, during the social and economic turmoil which ensued from the collapse of the

Soviet Union, a significant percentage of people across the country demonstrated against the government while carrying banners lionizing Stalin. They missed the order and control he imposed on them. They craved, not just strong leadership, but dictatorial domination. The abuses of state power that became so common during the 1990s under Boris Yeltsin's government didn't bother them at all.

Even as an expatriate living there I felt it. A few times a week I would be stopped by the traffic police as I drove to and from work. They usually said my license plates were dirty, an offense that could cost you a painful fine. But instead of letting the ticket wind its way through the Moscow bureaucracy, I would ask how much it would cost to "clean" them, and after handing the officer a few dollars he would let me go. Once, they got me when my visa had expired, an offence that could have lead to deportation if handled officially. As the officer prepared to impound my car I asked how much a "new" visa would cost. I slipped him a $50 bill and went on to work.

What sort of culture ignores the individual while granting the ruling elite unfettered power? Until the establishment of liberal democracy in the U.S. that was the norm worldwide. Nobody knew how to form a society without a monarch and an entrenched aristocracy. Whose views should be heard? And whose should be implemented? In the middle of the Revolutionary War, an English social reformer named Jeremy Bentham proposed a new framework to answer these questions, utilitarianism. Whichever policy produces the greatest happiness for the greatest number of people should be the policy adopted by a democratic state; in other words, majority rule.

Bentham would not have approved of the autocracy of Russia's long history, but at moments when the tsars acted in ways consistent with the majority view he would not have objected. But eighty years later, as our countrymen prepared to fight each other over the liberty of slaves, another English philosopher, John Stuart Mill, refined this idea. He explained that intellectual and moral pleasures rank higher than physical ones in their ability to produce happiness. Mill was an outspoken opponent of slavery, and concluded that the one thing most likely to foster intellectual and moral happiness is individual liberty. "The worth of the state," he explained, "...is the worth of the individuals composing it." In his view, individual liberty must be supreme and inviolable.

Mill had help reaching this conclusion. The Founding Fathers understood it almost a century earlier, and built it into the fabric of our democracy. Placing the individual's rights above all proved to be a popular foundation on which to build a nation. In the 231 years since the signing of the Declaration of Independence, the number of democracies in the world has grown from one to one hundred twenty-two. Now we take it for granted that we can do whatever we want as long as our choices don't harm anyone else. My first taste of Russian business became obsessively compelling. I wanted to get over there as fast as possible and build something of my own in the world's newest democracy.

After a few years trying to work in Russia from a cozy office in London, and a year-and-a-half in grad school in California, I moved to Moscow in 1995 to join my friends, Charlie Ryan and Boris Fedorov, with whom I had dreamed up a business plan to launch an investment bank. My first apartment, on Delegatskaya Street about a half-mile north of the Bolshoi Theater, was unimpressive. On the eighth floor of a ten-story apartment complex overlooking the stadiums where Russia had hosted the 1980 summer Olympic Games, it was furnished with a velour sofa and chair and hideous throw rugs on splintered parquet floors. The ground-floor lobby looked like a crack den, its wallpaper long since torn away and its cracked tile floor littered with old cigarette butts. The mailbox was dinged and rusted. The front door, a large and heavy metal slab, had probably not closed properly since Nikita Khrushchev's time as General Secretary of the Soviet Union; it rang like a gong every time its spring hinge slammed it shut.

Every morning I walked the half-mile to work at my office on Tverskaya Street, the main drag of Moscow running from Red Square out to the airport, and much further out to the town of Tver. My partners and I had set up shop in a converted apartment with four rooms and a little kitchen; a dive, really, with low-pile carpeting, plain white walls, and a phone. We brokered Russian stocks for investors in the U.S. and Western Europe. Charlie ran the show. He and I had known each other a little in college, and had shared a flat in London when we were both working there. Like me, Charlie is fiercely competitive. We planned to make our mark on the world, and never doubted that we could. Within the first year in Moscow we had booked millions of dollars' worth of trades, and I moved out of my shabby apartment. Under Charlie's leadership our firm grew to become the largest independent investment bank in the country.

Moscow then was full of prospectors like us, American and European guys in their twenties digging for the mother lode. Every night there was a party somewhere where a little booze would produce braggarts who couldn't keep their latest nugget a secret. So we went out every night with our ears perked up. One night, at a crowded party in the apartment of someone we barely knew, Charlie overheard a conversation: "Yadda yadda oil stocks blah blah blah San Antonio yadda yadda Dana so-and-so." It was just the break we were looking for. We left and hustled back to the office even though it was one in the morning because it was four in the afternoon in Texas. We called information in San Antonio and asked for San Antonio Asset Management. No such listing. San Antonio Partners. No such listing. San Antonio Capital? Yes! We dialed the number.

"San Antonio Capital, can I help you?" We asked for Dana.

"Can I ask what this is regarding?" she asked.

"Russian oil stocks."

"Hold, please."

Soon a guy got on the phone and said, "This is Dana."

We talked for thirty seconds, barely long enough to introduce ourselves, before he said he'd buy up to one million of such-and-such oil company at no more than $X per share. That was our first big break. Bingo, we were in business!

Building a profitable business in Moscow in the mid-1990s was the easy part. The greater challenge was getting accustomed to the standard of living. Russia then had a weak, eroded infrastructure, a country with muscle but a faltering command system, so it struggled and jerked as I do now, graceless yet determined. In the Moscow I knew, you couldn't count on your pipes to work, and when they did, they sometimes spewed rusty water so cold that showers were painful. The air was filthy. Drinking the tap water would give you a variety of intestinal infections. And there was no junk food – no Snap, Crackle, 'n Pop, no Kool Aid, no Doritos. Salami and potatoes were the standard fare. As a health-conscious American with a family history of heart disease, I was determined to stay in shape. In warm weather, I ran on the Moscow River embankment; in winter I worked out at a gym. I became a master of one-pot, one-utensil meals. Having found a German grocery store that stocked frozen chicken fingers, an Indian store that imported tikka masala sauce in a jar, and an Italian store that sold frozen pellets of chopped spinach, I could throw together a tasty and reasonably healthy dinner.

Sometimes a one-pot meal required unusual preparation methods. Because I wanted chicken pieces, not fingers, but didn't have the patience for thawing and chopping, I just pulled out a hammer and smashed them into bite size morsels. Then I would put

everything in the pot on a low boil, sit down on my velour sofa, read the Moscow Times, and sip a beer.

My parents visited me once in Moscow and
wondered why I insisted on living at a lower standard
than I might have chosen elsewhere. They were happy
to help me pay for a nicer place, but I craved independence every way I could get it. And I felt proud
that I had adapted to my new surroundings, that I could
prosper in such a forbidding environment.

One of my clients then was a shipping company
based in Goteborg, on the western coast of Sweden.
They wanted to invest in a shipyard in Muroam, a Russian town of 20,000 people located about 400 miles
east of Moscow. We agreed to visit the shipyard together to make sure investing was a good idea, so we
set a date. We had to take a train to get there; Muroam
had no airport. The trains going east always leave in
the evening so you can sleep and then arrive in the
middle of absolute nowhere early enough to spend a
whole day doing absolutely nothing except toasting to
mother Russia with a bottle of shpiert, 150-proof
vodka so raw they put flakes of dried garlic in it to
mask the flavor. Unfortunately, Muroam isn't far
enough away to sleep so we stayed up and arrived
around midnight.

We were met on the platform by the General
Director of the shipyard who escorted us to a sort of
bed-n-breakfast. In Russia it's considered rude not to
eat with guests, and even ruder not to accept the invitation, so at one o'clock in the morning we sat down to a
meal of chicken that tasted as if it had been butchered
a month earlier and boiled ever since with potatoes and

cabbage. I happily toasted the motherland a few times figuring that if I got drunk enough I wouldn't taste it. That was all it took because I have always been a lightweight. After dinner we bade farewell to the shipyard guy until morning and then the proprietor showed us to our room. That's room, singular, not rooms. They were booked completely. So my client and I were shown into a room about ten feet square with floor, walls and ceiling tiled in a pukey green, a toilet in one corner, and a pair of saggy cots.

Again I figured the booze in my veins would conquer all the issues raised by the charming accommodations. So I climbed in bed and tried to get some sleep. As visions of sugarplums began dancing in my head, the door opened. A rotund woman came in, flipped on the light, hiked up her dress, took a seat on the toilet, and opened her newspaper to catch up on the day's news. We weren't sleeping in a bathroom. We were sleeping in the bathroom, and had visitors all night.

Fortunately, Moscow hurtled into the post-Communist era hurriedly and excitedly, making nights spent in bathrooms more the exception than the rule. My partners and I were making money, but our lifestyles, at home and at work, did not reflect this. We preferred the cheap rents to fancy digs, the latter having been filled with the "New Russians," local entrepreneurs who made a fast buck in the first years of unfettered capitalism and were eager to show it. One memorable afternoon, however, we were stung by our own modesty. At about 2:30, we got a call from one of our clients in the U.S.; he was making an impromptu visit. He would be in Moscow in twenty hours and wanted to meet "the team." Our team then was five salespeople and a half-blind guy named Maxim who maintained our computer network. We hung up from our client's call, ran outside to a magazine seller and bought a dozen copies of a lousy stock market rag that had plenty of charts and graphs. We chopped them up and taped them all over the walls. And we set up computers all around the office to make it look like we had a big staff.

The next morning, the client called from the airport to say he was on his way. My partners and I scurried into work. When we arrived at our entrance we found a very drunk Russian man lying in front of the door, mumbling and cursing. It was February when the temperature rarely gets above twenty degrees. The drunk looked bad; blue lips, frozen fingers. He had obviously passed out there the night before. Our client was due in forty-five minutes. The collapsed man wouldn't let anyone touch him to carry him inside. So we called the police. The police said they wouldn't come because the drunk wasn't disturbing anyone. We called an ambulance service but they wouldn't come because we couldn't tell them the man's name. We called the city coroner's office but they wouldn't come because, well, he was alive. With only thirty minutes left, we were getting desperate. We bought a bottle of vodka to lure him inside or away, anywhere but in front of our door, but by the time we returned, the man had died.

"Hey Charlie, you still have the coroner's number?"

The agent from the coroner's office arrived fifteen minutes before our client was due. Tick, tock, tick, tock. We were getting nervous.

"Can we help you get him in your van?" we asked.

"No, he cannot be moved without police authorization," he replied. The police were on their way, he continued, but meanwhile he had to prep the corpse. Resigned to the inevitability that our client would encounter this strange spectacle, we stepped back to give the coroner some room. He stripped the poor guy naked and slathered some yellowish, greasy goop on him from head to toe. And as if it could not get more surreal with our precious client only minutes away, the dead guy had a huge hard-on.

Our client arrived, eager to determine whether he should continue to give his business to us. As if corpses lay on the doorstep of every stock brokerage, he stepped over the naked, greasy, aroused, dead guy without comment, and kept on walking, ready to get to work. He understood that the new economic landscape in Russia would be dotted with obstacles he couldn't foresee, but he also believed he could overcome them by focusing on what he had come to do. The obvious tragedy of a man who had died from drinking his way to oblivion during a frozen Moscow night may have affected him, perhaps even deeply, but he didn't let it break his stride because his goal mattered more to him than the process of achieving it. Like him, I have encountered countless obstacles as my strength and coordination have disappeared, but also like him I have learned to step over them on the way to something more important.

We, too, kept on walking. Our operations grew quickly. Within a year we had twenty-five people working at our firm, and that 1,000 square foot office became noisy and crowded. We moved into a refurbished mansion on a hill that overlooked the Moscow River to the east of the Kremlin. It was a yellow stucco building with three floors; we occupied most of the second. It had a gated courtyard and a fountain in front that was patrolled by security guards night and day. In eighteen months we outgrew that space, probably 6,000 square feet, as well. But by that time we had acquired a commercial bank which owned a brand new, seven-story building a half-mile north of Red Square where our team would have room to grow.

Life was hectic and fast paced, like stepping onto a treadmill spinning at full speed. Our team spent the early morning catching up on political and economic news while our clients in Western Europe were just getting out of bed. The trading day began around ten or eleven o'clock. We would report to our clients, find out which stocks they wanted to buy or sell. Then we would work the phones looking for the other side of the trade. By four o'clock in the afternoon, our clients in New York were just starting their day, so we'd continue to trade late into the evening. There wasn't time for much else. I dated someone for a few months, but I couldn't be with her and still work as hard as I wanted to.

There was one interlude, though. One lazy summer weekend my friends and I rented a skippered sailboat to float around the canal system that connects the Moscow River to points as far away as the upper Baltic Sea. The boat was about forty feet long with an inboard motor. We sailed past deep green woods of birch and passed an occasional dacha on the shore. We sipped barely cooled beers and munched on cheese and crackers. The air was warm, the northern sunlight muted by gigantic, puffy clouds. I lay on the boat's edge and trailed my hand in the water. Despite the jabbering of my friends, everything was very quiet. I could feel the gentle breeze on my face, and hear my heart beating slowly. And what happened, I wondered, between each beat? I had once heard someone say a heart beats two billion times in an average life span. If you were to add them up, how many moments are there between beats? Can you make a sum of silences?

Eve Tetzlaff began working in the office in January 1997. By then our firm had grown big enough for me to launch a venture capital department. Eve was perfect for the job. She had a degree from Yale, had worked at McKinsey & Company, the largest management consulting firm in the world, and spoke Russian flawlessly. I had met her when she interviewed in November, and tried not to focus on a crucial detail left out of her resume: Eve was beautiful – long blond hair, turquoise eyes, petite, and a bright affecting smile.

I had long since outgrown the shy, tongue-tied crush of my teenage summer in Greece, and had dated now and then, even thought I had fallen in love once.

But I was Eve's boss. I tried to keep my manner cool and levelheaded but her smile filled the office we shared. She laughed at my jokes, chimed in with her own; we saw humor in the same things.

Soon, our laughter became heightened and charged. I was too aware of where she was in the office. I missed her when she left for lunch. At home, away from work, I would tell myself, "Jack, don't cross that line. She's an employee." But every morning when I came to work, there was Eve at her desk, tucking her hair behind her ears, talking on the phone, laughing, both of us trying not to meet the other's eye, neither of us succeeding.

On a chilly Friday in the first week of February we went to an Indian restaurant after work. Over papadams and chutney we saw each other differently than we had seen at the office. She wasn't my employee; I wasn't her boss. After we paid the bill I wondered what to do. Should I try to kiss her? That bright, white line I had told myself not to cross had faded to black. In my car on the way back into the city-center, I realized we would drive by my apartment building. As we got closer the conversation in my head became a raucous debate. I turned into the courtyard and parked the car.

"Where are we?" Eve asked. She had gotten lost in the winding city streets but knew we weren't near her apartment.

"My building," I answered. "Would you like…"

"Oh…yes, I would like to come in."

I had made it so complicated in my thoughts when it was really so simple, two people attracted to each other. But I held on to the complexity, and insisted we keep it a secret from my partners. Each night I would leave work and head home, and Eve would wait twenty minutes before catching a cab over. By then I had moved into a spacious, clean apartment on the Frunzenskaya embankment with a view of the Moscow River. Built originally by Stalin to house the Communist party elite, it had a brand new bathroom with its own water heater, a highly coveted item. It was the perfect place for a romance. We spent evenings eating my one-pot concoctions, listening to music, and talking for hours. Soon we were spending all of our free time together.

During my years working and traveling abroad I called my parents in St. Louis two or three times a month no matter where I was.

"Hey there!" I'd say when they answered the phone.

"Hi Boy!" my Dad would say. "Where are you?"

"I'm in Stockholm for a meeting tomorrow. Water, water everywhere, and nothing to eat but pickled herring."

"Haha! Well don't choke on the bones! Let me get your mom on the phone too. Lois! It's Jacko…"

They enjoyed living vicariously through my adventures, and I liked telling them my tales. But I never discussed my private life with them, or anyone really. It was simply off-limits.

"Are you meeting any girls?" my Dad asked.

"Well I am in Sweden you know, blondes everywhere."

I never gave them a straight answer. The same was true when Eve and I were dating, and it caused some funny moments. In January 1998, the Clinton/Lewinsky scandal broke. My Mom and I often discussed politics, and when she said, "Carrying on a relationship with a subordinate is inexcusable," I snickered quietly while holding my hand over the mouthpiece.

"Absolutely, Mom, couldn't agree more."

On Friday evenings Eve and I often went to hear the Moscow Philharmonic play at the Moscow Conservatory. The expatriate crowd we knew, mainly brokers and fund managers, generally spent their weekend evenings in Moscow's thriving clubs and casinos, so at the Conservatory I felt no need to hide. The tickets cost about eighty cents. We would listen to the music in the hall where centuries of Russians had felt the passion and suffering of their heritage, and pretty soon my hand would creep onto her leg. She would turn and smile at me, cast her eyes down modestly, and place her hand on mine. The music brought us closer, especially when the performance would include a piece we listened to in my apartment. Among other things I had a beautiful piano concerto by Rachmaninov which we played over and over again. Then one night at the Conservatory we watched candidates in the annual Tchaikovsky Competition, many of whom chose the Rachmaninov concerto as their optional piece, bring our CD to life. We listened for our favorite passages, attuned to one another's breathing, our bodies in time to the violins and cellos on stage.

Unfortunately, the unrestrained affection we could share at the Conservatory was hard to find elsewhere with my secretiveness in tow like a ball-and-chain. Right or wrong, I did not want our relationship to become office gossip. I was jockeying with one of my partners to run a new department in the company, and I didn't want anyone to question my professional ethics. But it annoyed Eve and occasionally strained our relationship. A few times it led to a breakup.

"It's not right," I would say. "This just proves how bad an idea it is for us to be involved, I think we should stop."

She would get upset, and I would apologize, and then we would talk some more, and agree not to see each other. We would honor our agreement for a week or so. I felt lonely without her in my spacious apartment, but I told myself the decision was the right one. But I kept seeing her at the office, her dazzling smile, and we still had to talk to one another because no one knew we had been dating, or had now broken off. When we talked to each other we started to joke around and have fun again, and before long I would find myself walking through the city at night, pretending I wasn't going to Eve's place but always ending up hitting the buzzer at the entrance to her building.

"Hello?"

"Hi, it's me. Can I come up?"

"Uhm, sure." She knew what I had come to say. In her apartment we'd sit on the plush sofa in her living room.

"I'm sorry, I know I'm jerking you around. At work I get so caught up in the politics, and it seems like the right thing to do. But then as soon as I leave I'm lonely for you and I realize I've made a mistake."

"It's OK Jack. You want a glass of wine?" We might have continued that cycle but for the intervention of the Russian government. On August 16, 1998, exactly seven years after my first trip to Moscow, the government devalued the ruble to keep the Central Bank from going broke. That meant that everyone holding ruble-denominated government bonds saw their investments dive to just kopeks. The entire banking system ground to a halt. Most of my stake in the firm my partners and I had built was in the investment fund I was managing at the time and the new one I was raising. The investors in both scurried away like bugs on a cabin floor when you flip on the light. With them went my reason to stay in Russia.

Eve and I packed up and headed for San Francisco, where I had high hopes and sketchy plans for participating in the dot-com craze. We hoped our relationship would normalize if we were no longer employer and employee as well as lovers. I bought a tony loft near downtown and Eve rented an apartment in the Castro district a few miles away. The first month there felt odd for me. We were thousands of miles from Moscow, but when I looked at Eve I still saw my employee. I still saw someone who would do, essentially, what I asked, who would defer to my judgment, and who depended upon me in many ways. I didn't want that, but I felt like Sisyphus pushing our ten-ton history up a hill only to lose my grip and watch it crash

47

down the path I had taken. It seemed futile to ignore that boulder. If I did it would have crushed me.

Once again I broke things off, and once again I spent a miserable month without her. Then one evening she invited me out to dinner to meet a friend of hers from college days. We met at Eve's apartment, and then I drove the three of us to the restaurant. Filled with good food and wine, we all had a great time, more fun than I'd had since...well, the last time I was with Eve. The pattern was so obvious. As her friend went to the ladies' room I put my arm around Eve and stroked her back. Why else had she invited me to dinner if not to draw me back into a relationship? But she pulled away.

"I thought we were 'just friends,'" she said as she twisted free.

"Well, I thought so too, but then you invited me to dinner, and we had such a great time...so, what do you think?" I said.

For the first time she didn't smile and say, "Oh, Jack, it's okay." Something had changed in her; I could see it in her posture and in the level way she met my eyes. "I'll think about it," she said. And then her friend returned.

As we drove away I felt stunned. I'll think about it? She, Eve, my employee, no, my former employee, was calling the shots? How foolish I had been to think she would always take me back. I thought it was my decision whether or not we would be together.

Eve agreed a few days later to meet at her apartment and talk. She met me at my car on the street in front of her building, hair tied back, no make-up;

she looked severe. She got in and turned toward me silently.

"If I'm going to take you back it has to be different than it's been, Jack." She stared straight at me. I had seen that look before, when we would visit one of the companies in which we had invested through my venture capital fund. It was the look she got when I told her I wanted the management of the company to feel like they were getting a stiff kick in the ass, and she was good at it. "No more hiding. No more secretiveness. No more of your self-flagellating nonsense about your so-called ethics. I'm not falling for that anymore, Jack. You think you have so much integrity going, but it's just a smokescreen for common male commitment phobia."

Her words hit me smack in the stomach.

"I want a relationship between equals, between two partners," she said. "I don't want a supervisor for a boyfriend. I want a partner."

"That's what I want, too," I finally said. And it was true. That was what bothered me most, that we had not been equals.

Six months later, in August 1999, we went to northern Wisconsin to stay for two weeks with Eve's parents at their summer cottage. It was the first real vacation we had taken together. We swam, tanned, fished, and canoed. We ate blocks of sharp cheddar and homemade blueberry pie, and lay on the dock after dark looking at the stars. Was it the vast sky above, the sense I had of a limitless universe in which I had a small part to play? Was it the sun that warmed our backs, or the cool lake water that soothed them? Or was it a sense I had even then that I would need her? Whatever it was, I decided in Wisconsin that I would ask Eve to marry me.

Neither of us was the type to enjoy an elaborate scheme like freezing a ring in an ice cube. In September, in St. Louis, we climbed into bed in the room that had been mine as a boy, and we began to talk about marriage. We had weathered some difficult times and still our feelings for each other were strong. We didn't talk about children, not then. Years before, when I had worked in New York, one of the guys I worked for told me that the best thing he and his wife ever did was to enjoy married life without children for four or five years. I thought that sounded smart. I had always wanted children, and I thought there would be time for that with Eve. I saw myself forming a life partnership with this woman I had tried to stay away from and could not, this woman who had walked into my office with her flawless Russian and made me see that I was not exactly who I thought I was; this woman whom I loved, lying next to me, her shadow in my boyhood bedroom huge, substantial, and soft on the white wall.

We got engaged.

We were married on May 18, 2000, in Occidental, California, a tiny town up in the Sonoma wine country about three hours north of San Francisco where giant redwoods grow near the Russian River. The ceremony took place in the garden of a refurbished Victorian mansion, now a bed-and-breakfast. We kept the wedding small, only family. We had a non-denominational ceremony that I made sure was stripped of every romantic cliché, and every vapid clause. The ceremony lasted seven minutes, during which time my eleven-month-old nephew, Ethan Orchard, cried, and my five-year-old nephew, Drew Hoffman, dropped the rings as he delivered them from my sister Connie, his mother. Our families laughed with these adorable children, and my brother Harry, with his baby-boy drooling on him while sitting on his shoulders, remarked that it wouldn't be a real wedding unless something happened to foil the original plan.

I had wanted my wedding to be casual that way, as unscripted as possible, with good food and close family. We wrote our own vows. Eve promised, among other things, to scratch my bald spot to promote new hair growth. I promised not to get annoyed when she'd return from a trip and leave her bag unpacked on the bedroom floor for a week. At the time these promises were funny, and everyone chuckled, but in hindsight I see a different story starting. Eve's vows focused on what she would do for me, whereas mine said I wouldn't get irritated with who she was, or what she had to give. She was ready to embrace our new life together, but I hadn't adapted to the idea yet.

The Virgin Mary appeared to a woman in Florida in an unlikely place, the burn marks of her grilled cheese sandwich. She was so convinced it was a sign that she kept it for a decade before auctioning it on eBay for $28,000. Evolutionary biologists explain the tendency to see faces in unlikely places as an adaptation that greatly enhances our chances of survival – the cost of not recognizing the face of a predator hiding in the bushes is far higher than the cost of falsely recognizing a face in clouds, on the surface of Mars, or the flipside of a grilled cheese sandwich.

We have adapted to recognize faces just as we have adapted countless other traits in humankind's steady march to supremacy over the other species with which we share our planet. Adaptability is the source of our strength in unfamiliar places and circumstances, whether sleeping in bathrooms or stepping over frozen men or learning to live with paralysis. When I look back on my years in Russia I see my face painted on Matryoshki nesting dolls, one inside the other, each one a surprise, each one smaller, younger, and less flexible than the last. I see eyes laughing when they could have cried, and bags under them packed with patience. And though I know those faces, those eyes, the younger of them I don't easily recognize, and I'm glad of it.

Chapter Four

Forced Vital Capacity

◆◆◆◆◆◆◆

Who has never had a muscle twitch or cramp? After a long day at the office staring at computer screens you get a little wiggle in the tiny muscles around your eye. Or you run a little further than you usually do, and after sitting at the end with a big jar of Gatorade your calf tightens into a knot. It happens so often you probably can't remember the last time it happened to you. But then your health changes, and you can't help but wonder if every change, big and small, is connected to every other one. You strain to remember every instance a muscle behaved unusually.

In college, during my first meeting with my senior thesis advisor, an eminent economist who was reputed to shred undergraduates before devouring them, I remember having difficulty speaking, as if my cheeks somehow got in the way of my mouth while it attempted to spit out words. As inexplicably as it happened, it never happened again. A few years later, in the early 1990s after a ski vacation, my right foot went limp mysteriously, and then, three days later, went back to normal. And another time, while in Moscow, I put my arms around Eve and felt the muscles around my shoulder blades seize up. As I began to experience the symptoms of my illness, I couldn't help but wonder if all these events were related.

My creeping paralysis was at first indistinguishable from the sensations of everyday life, the muscles' small mistakes. I was turning a doorknob and it felt strangely new, as though I had never turned one before. Unlike the other muscular miscues years earlier, however, this new sensation recurred. At the time, Eve and I were living in my loft near downtown San Francisco. With three levels and a great view of the city skyline from a deck on the roof, it satisfied my hunger for an improved lifestyle after all those years in Russia. So what if my hand felt odd? I tried to dismiss it as insignificant.

Something I thought was similar had happened ten years earlier, in the spring of 1990, when I had gone skiing at Lake Tahoe with one of my college roommates. It was only the second time I had ever skied and the rental clerk unwittingly gave me a pair of stiff, slalom skis, inappropriate for the slushy spring show. I banged down the mogul-covered hills, unaware that the skis were too stiff to absorb much of the shock. Instead, my lumbar vertebrae took it all. After that ski trip, I endured back pain for three years before a stinging pain in my knees finally sent me to my internist, who sent me to a sports therapist, who sat me on his exam table. I couldn't straighten my legs without feeling pain in the knees. Then the sports doctor helped me to sit up tall on his exam table with my back straight as a marine's. I lifted my feet again and felt not even a hint of pain in my knees.

"Jack, your knees are fine, but your back is an issue," he said. I had herniated a disk, he explained, and a disk rupture can put pressure on the nerves running down the legs. He gave me a book explaining various exercises I could do to repair the rupture, a referral to a neurosurgeon if the exercises didn't relieve the pain, and he suggested giving up skiing.

Doing my back exercises I found I could repair a rupture, or at least eliminate the pain I felt, in a matter of weeks. So I didn't give up skiing. In fact, I took to the mountains as often as I could, addicted as I was to the sensation of the wind whipping through my hair and the burn in my legs after an intense run. Occasionally, I would take a nasty spill and rupture the disk again, and I accepted the discomfort during the recovery as the price I needed to pay to support my habit. Like a drug addict, it was inevitable I would overdose eventually. Over New Year's 1997 I was skiing with friends in Colorado when it ruptured again, this time so painfully that I scheduled an emergency visit to the neurosurgeon in St. Louis before I had to return to Moscow.

"It's a serious injury," he said. "If you were an older man I'd book you for surgery to remove the herniated disk and fuse together the vertebrae above and below it."

"Why would I have to be older?" I asked.

"Because any time you work on the spinal column there is a risk that the nerves in the spinal cord may get damaged. There's about a five percent chance that everything below the point of the diskectomy would get knocked out, everything. If you were in your fifties with as many children as you wanted, this would be a viable option, but at your age you'd be gambling with your chance to have a family, your career..."

"So what do you think I should do?"

"Let's see how you feel in a few months after following your exercise regimen. And hang up your skis for good, or the next time you're in here you'll be in a wheelchair, and nobody will be able to fix it." I sold my skis the next day, and exercised my way back to having minimal pain. But unlike in the past, it never went away completely.

Now, I blamed the new sensation in my hand on that old back injury. If a herniated disk could make my knees hurt, why couldn't it affect my hand too? In late 1999 I was on the phone with my parents and mentioned the strange feeling in my left hand. My Mom called a neurologist friend they knew in St. Louis who agreed to squeeze me into his calendar in two days, after his Friday appointments.

The doctor put me through the rather mundane steps of a neurological exam. He demonstrated a variety of motions he wanted to see me perform. We started with my right side. Spread my fingers apart, then squeeze them together. Touch my thumb to each fingertip. Tap my index finger on my thumb as quickly as I can. Lift up my toes. Tap my foot as quickly as I can. Stand on my toes, then on my heels.

On my right side I could do everything with the same dexterity he could. But when I tried to tap my left index finger to my thumb, it wouldn't move as quickly as my right index finger had done. I felt a flood of adrenaline. My skin tingled all over my body. I put both hands up and tried to tap side by side. My left was simply slower, as if it were submerged in quicksand, the slurry holding my fingers from moving as quickly as they would have in open air. WHAT THE HELL?!? Stunned and frightened, I looked in the doctor's eyes for a cue. I thought if he's not worried there's no reason I should be worried either, right? But he kept a neutral look on his face, utterly dispassionate.

When he finished examining me he made a few notes and then began asking questions. Had I ever been tested for AIDS? Did I ever have unprotected sex? Had I been heavily exposed to pesticides or other sources of heavy metals? Did I feel any tingling in my extremities? Had I ever shared a needle to take drugs? Did I feel any pain in my ankles or knees? Had I experienced any tremors? Had I experienced any memory loss?

On and on the questions came, but at last it was my chance to ask one. "Could my back injury be the source of the problem?"

Not a chance. A herniated disk in the lower back could affect your legs, he explained, but not your arms. "You have the body of a young man in good shape," he went on, "but your left hand is like that of a seventy-year old man."

"A seventy-year old man?! What does that mean?" I nearly shouted.

He only threw up his hands and said: "There could be dozens of explanations."

"Like...?" I heard my voice becoming edgy. I wanted, if not answers, at least information. In Moscow, surrounded by chaos, I had made decisions about other people's money by gathering bits of information. Now, when I might have to make decisions concerning my own body, I had nothing to work with. I needed information.

"It could be nothing more than a case of pinched nerves," he said, "Or, it could be more serious. The blood work we're doing should narrow the possibilities, and some other tests will narrow them further."

"You said dozens of explanations. That's only one."

He didn't answer right away, but looked at me as if I had overstepped the courtesy he had extended to me by seeing me on such short notice. Then he sighed, and ticked off a list on his fingers. "AIDS, Lyme disease, mercury poisoning, multiple sclerosis, Parkinson's disease, Huntington's disease, Creutzfeld-Jacob disease, spinal muscular atrophy, myasthenia gravis, Friedrich's ataxia, Charcot-Marie-Tooth disease...Jack, we just don't know yet. Let's not jump to conclusions."

Apparently, he had given me enough of his time that day. His lips pursed shut. He reached across the space between his desk and the exam table on which I sat, and handed me a set of papers with orders for various tests. He stood up, shook my hand, and said, "I'll see you Monday, and call you when the blood results are in."

Soon a nurse entered with a tray full of vials. I held out my right arm, the good one. She tied a rubber tube around my bicep and tapped on the crease in my elbow. I wore a wool sweater which itched my arm while the nurse scrubbed my skin with an alcohol-soaked cotton swab. Two hours earlier I had been ready to face back surgery, maybe spend a couple days in the hospital and a few weeks recuperating, but now I had entered a nightmare, which, if I had understood the doctor, could go on indefinitely. The nurse readied her needle and plunged it into the bulging blue vein she had coaxed. I watched my dark red blood spurt into vial after vial. Which was the vial for AIDS? Which one for Lyme disease?

I walked out of there profoundly shaken, my arm sore from the phlebotomist's needle. How could I just go home and pretend everything was normal for a few days while my future flapped in the breeze like an old sheet hung up to dry? Back at my parents' home I called Eve in San Francisco. She was still at work but I needed to talk. I told her what the doctor had said, how I had gotten frightened, and asked her to come wait with me until my tests Monday morning.

Before Eve arrived my mind had raced ahead asking questions. If it's no big deal, why would a busy doctor make room in his schedule on short notice to see me? Didn't that mean he thought it was potentially serious? And how about all of those diseases he mentioned?

Eve's presence brought me back to reality. Most of the diseases the doctor mentioned are so uncommon that the odds of having any of them were virtually nil. Creutzfeld-Jacob disease is the human variant of mad cow disease, which has only occurred a few dozen times around the entire world in the last decade.

"You're right," I said. "Of course you're right. It's ridiculous to think it could be serious when there's probably a simple explanation."

"So quit imagining the worst when the truth is probably no big deal!" she said.

On Monday morning we reported to the hospital's MRI lab, fully decompressed after a weekend's worth of relaxation. MRI is a process in which a machine sends radio waves through some part of the body, and catches them on the way out. By analyzing how the waves are bent by the tissues through which they pass, the machine can draw a picture of the body part's internal structure, particularly the soft tissues that do not show up in an x-ray. This procedure takes about fifteen minutes lying very still as the machine whirrs, pops, pings, and clangs.

Then we were led into another room for the electromyogram, a test used to detect pinched nerves or a nerve injury, such as carpel tunnel syndrome. While lying as still and relaxed as I could, a nurse attached small electrodes at two points on each limb and on my back, and then ran electric shocks between them while measuring how quickly the pulse traveled from one electrode to the other. Then she stabbed a needle electrode through my skin into the muscles of my thighs and upper arms, and twisted it to generate an electrical response in the muscle tissue itself, one that could be measured. During this painful exam Eve and I cracked jokes about how medieval it seemed, a throwback to an era when blistering and leeches were considered effective medical treatments.

Back in the doctor's office, he met with us to review the test results. The MRI had revealed a bulging disk in my neck but he dismissed it as being too minor to create the unusual action in my left hand. And the electromyogram had found a minor diminution of nerve conductivity in my left arm but nothing strictly abnormal anywhere. Although it seemed like good news to be pronounced in good shape, the doctor appeared more concerned, not less.

"I thought that finding nothing wrong would be good news," I said.

"Ordinarily it would be. But the MRI and EMG revealed that it may not have a simple answer such as a pinched nerve. I'll have the blood results in a few days. In the meantime, you should find a neurologist out in San Francisco for a follow-up visit in three months."

The angst I had felt before Eve had arrived suddenly infected both of us. We had collected a handful of brochures from the waiting room and sat in a park across from the hospital reading them. Panic was one symptom listed for advanced Lyme disease, and I certainly was experiencing panic. Did I have any of Lyme disease's other symptoms such as painful joints or hyperacusis, a severe sensitivity to sound and vibration? A bird on a branch was chirping awfully loudly. And what about Creutzfeldt-Jacob disease, in which case I would have a year left to live and could look forward to hallucinations and dementia? Eve reminded me there was no reason to suspect I had AIDS. But what about Huntington's rapid jerking movements, called chorea, from the Greek word for dance? If I had

Huntington's disease I could have twenty more dancing years but I would lose my mind. In such a moment of madness, which would you pick if you had to pick one, a condition in which you would keep your faculties but die quickly, or one in which you would lose them so slowly that you might never understand what you've lost?

By the time we had finished reading about the possible diagnoses that might explain the sensations in my hand, we hoped I had multiple sclerosis; it usually has a slow progression, remissions, and normal expected lifespan. I was struck by the absurdity of it all. Three days earlier I had been hoping for a million-dollar deal, and now I was hoping for a slow road to death. Luck is entirely relative.

Back in California, I felt panicky, hot and cold at the same time, unable to concentrate. Eve was working at a dot-com company in Los Altos, fifty miles south in Silicon Valley, so she was up and gone early each morning, leaving me alone to stew in my imagination all day. From her books she had pulled a thin paperback about meditation before she left. "This could really help you to relax," she wrote on a sticky note stuck to its cover, "It's about clearing your mind." I badly needed something to do. Because I was scared, I deliberately stayed away from going online to do my own research. I didn't want to know about the diseases he mentioned, not yet at least. And I respected the man in the white coat, his impressive degrees and medical experience. Hadn't he warned about jumping to conclusions?

No matter what I told myself, I was tense during those days. I wanted to hear the doctor say that my red count or white count was abnormal and causing my problems. I wanted him to prescribe a pill I could take to bring me back to the normal person I knew myself to be. My heart thumped so loudly I felt like the protagonist of the *Tell-Tale Heart*, deafened and maddened by the rhythmic beat.

When the phone rang it was a perfectly beautiful afternoon. "Your blood work is fine," said the neurologist in his falsely neutral voice. "You appear to be perfectly healthy."

Blessed, lucky words for sure, but I knew, and the doctor knew, that this was the worst news I could have had. He reminded me to see a neurologist in San Francisco for another exam in three months to see if my symptoms had progressed. Ironically, in my case, progression meant deterioration. Progress – that American ideal to which I had always subscribed – now meant my demise.

I called my sister whose close friend is a renowned pediatrician in the Bay Area. She asked him who he thought was a good neurologist in the area. He recommended Dr. Robert Miller, a clinician and research scientist, and one of the most eminent neurologists in the country. I made an appointment for early May, just a few weeks before our wedding.

During the intervening months I constantly queried parts of my body. Was that spasm in my upper back longer than it should be? My foot fell asleep and the tingling spread up my leg—surely that was a bad sign? After relentless observation, I could not find any change in the strength of my right arm and legs, which I took as a good sign. But I was pretty certain I had felt my left arm change. The strange sensation I had felt in my left hand had morphed into obvious weakness, and the muscles in my forearm now routinely tightened into a cramp any time I squeezed something.

Finally the appointed day came. I parked near the neurologist's office, which happens to be located on a steep hill. As I opened the door to his office I felt short of breath. "Is it just anxiety?" I thought, "Or is it from the climb? And if it's the climb, why am I panting when I've scaled much more challenging terrain than this without getting winded?" I went alone, figuring that if I didn't make it into a big deal the results would be equally insignificant. As I came through the entrance, I passed a woman slumped down in her chair with her head resting forward on her chest like a crash test dummy, and a treacly line of drool stretching from her lips to her sweater. The office walls were covered with images of Lou Gehrig. There was a poster with the ALS Bill of Rights. I had not realized I had come to an ALS clinic as well as a general neurological office, and suddenly I felt frightened. In the waiting room were more patients; thin and stiff, their gait bizarrely dragging, their speech slurred. I stared into a magazine, trying to ignore the others waiting to be seen.

When the receptionist called my name I followed a neurology resident to a small examination room where he put me through the same tests the doctor in St. Louis had. Spread this, close that. Tap this, tap that. Rise on demi-pointe, pirouette, jeté, and bow.

Next, my breathing capacity. Into a small gadget that looked like a clunky 1970s calculator, another white-coat plugged a tube with a mouthpiece, then entered my height, weight, and age. This was to calculate my expected breathing capacity. Then he clipped shut my nose and told me to blow all the air of out my lungs. When I had reached the furthest point I could go, he stuck the mouthpiece in and I sucked in air as much and as quickly as I could. Then I blew it all the way back out. The amount of air I inhaled and exhaled, in technical terms, is called forced vital capacity. Then this amount is compared to the expected breathing capacity. This test is performed at least three times to eliminate errors like not getting a good seal on the mouthpiece, or not getting it in my mouth at exactly the right time. That first visit, my FVC was 5.3 liters, 100% of the expected amount. But in my disquiet, I felt decidedly short of breath.

Finally, it was time for a few words with the eminent neurologist. He looked through the notes the resident had written, and asked if there had been any changes since my exam in St. Louis. I explained what I had felt in my left arm.

"I'd like to expand on the blood tests from St. Louis," he said. "The weakness in your left arm can also result from an auto-immune disorder. To address it we could look at gamma globulin therapy. It's basically a way to give your immune system a temporary boost. First, let's do some more blood tests."

Despite my usual optimistic approach to everything, I had gotten spooked by what I had seen in the waiting room, and just had to ask about the worst-case scenario. "Does it look like ALS?" I muttered. I could not fathom that I had come up against a situation resistant to my typical analytical approach.

"ALS is almost always diagnosed by exclusion, by testing negative for many other conditions that can mimic its symptoms, and by the progression of symptoms unique to ALS. We'll have to see if that left hand weakness progresses to the right side and lower body because an ALS diagnosis requires impairment in all extremities."

"And when will that be? How long does that usually take?"

"Well, after all the time since your tests in St. Louis, to present with such minor symptoms now would be unusual. The disease course in ALS generally involves a fast progression." He evaded answering my question directly, but his response soothed my concerns for the moment.

A few weeks later I received a bill from Dr. Miller's office. I assumed it was the co-pay for my visit, and tore open the envelope. I owed nearly $600 for a one-hour visit. My insurance company had rejected the claim because I had already seen a physician for the same problem. "So what?" I thought. I had done exactly what the first doctor had instructed me to do. How could the insurer just reject the claim? I dug through my files and found the number for Blue Cross / Blue Shield of California. After a short wait I spoke with a customer service representative. She explained that my policy covered only single visits to doctors and emergency medical care. Because the follow-up visit had not been "necessary" my policy didn't cover it.

"How can I upgrade my policy to cover more?"
I asked.

"You can certainly apply for a more comprehensive policy," she answered, "but with an indeterminate, pre-existing medical condition, your chances of getting approved by the underwriters are pretty low." From that point on, every appointment, every test, every tap, pull, squeeze, and lift, would all come right out of my pocket.

My hand was ill but my career was thriving. I had plenty of work in which to bury myself while I waited for my blood work results from Dr. Miller. My sister, Connie, and I were in the process of putting together a new venture capital fund. She had built and run Pulitzer Technologies, the information technology division of Pulitzer Inc., at that time an independent, medium-sized newspaper, radio, TV, and Internet company. As part of my plan to reinvent myself from a Russian fund manager to a Silicon Valley venture capitalist, I had taken on a consulting assignment with Pulitzer to advise them while they invested in new media. Connie spent many months trying to convince Pulitzer to commit a large amount of money to internet-based companies and technologies until she concluded they just were not going to be as aggressive about it as she thought they should be.

One day, she and I were discussing this, and we hatched a plan. We would team up and build an investment fund for young companies in the Midwest that had exciting technologies. Connie, who was living in St. Louis, knew the media business, especially where it intersected with the Internet, better than anyone in the Midwest. With her experience building and managing the kinds of companies in which we would invest, and my experience building and managing venture capital funds, our endeavor seemed promising. We called our fund iSpringboard and we rented an office in St. Louis. Now it seems the name was no accident. I picture a man on a diving board, arcing up and then down into a pool as smooth as glass, his body sharp, supple, and perfectly controlled as he cuts into the water. Can a name create its referent? Had I hoped to call my healthy self into being?

Eve and I talked often in long rambling conversations. We were both frightened by the deterioration of my health, but up until then, we had chosen to focus on the other things in our lives. I had been flying around the country with my sister, meeting with prospective clients, and every night I phoned Eve. I looked forward to these long-distance conversations; we were frank and forthright, silly and playful, and I think we both gained a new appreciation for the other. We felt in synch with each other. We told ourselves that we were both optimistic, self-confident people, which we were, and that no matter what my symptoms might turn out to be we could address the problem and then move on.

Eve wanted to get a dog. She had been talking about a dog for months. Wouldn't it be fun to have a dog? Look at all the great dogs we see in the park every day. Why didn't I want to get a dog? Now her desire for a dog seemed to sharpen, but I didn't feel the same way about it. Dogs that slobbered or licked or made a mess annoyed me. Polite dogs that observed proper boundaries, chased a ball gracefully, and then sat waiting patiently for me to throw the ball again were enjoyable enough. But I had not wanted the burden of a dog I would have to walk and train, whose deposits I would have to clean up.

Now I began to consider the possibility of a dog. Maybe a dog would be a comfort to us. I began to watch the dogs in the park; they seemed infectiously happy with the sheer pleasure of running. I watched people jogging with their dogs, the two-legged jogger trying to keep up with the four-legged trotter, their muscles ceaselessly working. I saw a squirrel leap from one tree to another, soaring effortlessly through the air, and then run down the tree trunk and across the grass. I saw a cat rise up on its hind legs and bat at a yellow butterfly. I saw a stream run over rocks, the water clear and colorless; clouds drifting silently overhead, puffy and soft; trees swaying in the wind, all dancing in unison. I felt then how everything is made up of movement, of hidden muscles in motion, as though beneath the earth's skin there is a subcutaneous layer of ever active muscles, smooth and supple, contracting, stretching, all coordinated.

My second visit to Dr. Miller's clinic was on August 8, just three days before my 34th birthday. This time, hoping to make the walk easier, I parked uphill from the office building, only to find that walking down a steep hill was just as anxiety-provoking as walking up. In the waiting room there seemed to be even more disabled people in wheelchairs than I remembered. I watched a man shuffle across the room, his arms flapping against his sides. His wife guided him to the receptionist's window. His mouth hung open. Saliva dripped down his chin too quickly for his wife to catch. He looked about forty. For a second I couldn't breathe. It was too close. He might as well have been wearing a sandwich board that said: "This is your future."

The neurological exam included all the previous terrors – tap, tap, tap, rise up on my toes, walk down the hall, walk up the hall – and then, when my wits were fried, I was treated to "the rack." The rack is the hideous offspring conceived during a drunken encounter between a four-post bed and an all-in-one universal gym. It has handles and levers and wires strung all about. A neurology resident strapped me into the rack, and proceeded to isolate this or that muscle group. The cables attached to a gauge which attached to a computer which printed out the strength of each muscle group; biceps, triceps, quadriceps, hamstring.

This first time in the rack was to get my baseline measurements, the doctor explained. In three months, he would compare my muscle strength against today's results to give us an idea of any deterioration, uhm, progression. I was starting to catch on. Every quarter, I would be pulled, squeezed, walked, and tapped. Once again the neurology resident clipped shut my nose. I exhaled all the breath in my lungs and then sucked in as much as I could of that conditioned air. Once again, the resident duly calculated my forced vital capacity.

Later, I learned you can cry all you want about your biceps no longer working or your gait changing, but the only number that matters is your inevitably diminishing FVC. When it gets below half of the expected amount, you need to check your blood gases regularly to make sure you are getting enough oxygen to feed your hungry brain and tissues, and that you are expelling enough carbon dioxide to keep your blood below toxic levels. When it gets below twenty-five percent you should probably be using a ventilator at night. Below ten percent you will probably need one full-time.

At that visit the doctor asked me again what changes I had experienced, if any. I described how my right arm had begun cramping, and how I had felt an unusual sensation in my legs, a stiffening – too often to dismiss as coincidence – when I got out of the shower and stood in the chilly bathroom. And after any exertion the muscles on my thighs would twitch gently, like worms wiggling under a sheet. He explained that spasticity, the medical term for muscle stiffness, could result from deterioration of upper motor neurons, those connecting the brain to the spinal cord. To investigate further he had me sit on an exam table with my legs at rest dangling over the edge.

"Another symptom of upper motor neuron deterioration is heightened reflexes," he explained. Using a small hammer with a rubber head he gently tapped a spot on the front of my knee just below the kneecap. Instead of the slight reaction I expected, the quadriceps muscles on the top of my thigh jerked sharply. My leg kicked out almost completely horizontally, and then

71

fell back with a thud as my heel banged against the table. WHAT'S WRONG WITH ME?!?

"An ALS diagnosis requires deterioration in both the upper and lower motor neurons," he said. "Because of the original arm weakness which is a symptom of lower motor neuron deterioration, and the spasticity and hyperreflexivity in the legs," he said, "we might have to consider the possibility this is ALS."

Again I felt breathless. "Do you feel that definitively?" I asked.

"No," he said. "Not yet, but I can't ascribe your symptoms to any alternate cause."

"What about the gamma globulin therapy you described the last time I was here?"

"Well, at that time your symptoms were only in the one arm, but now that you have evidence of motor neuron loss in all four limbs, the auto-immune condition I was thinking about is clearly not the culprit."

So there it was, the diagnosis by exclusion. He could not positively call it ALS, so he ruled out everything else. More than 5,000 people in the United States go through the same nightmare every year, a new person on death row every ninety minutes. The full name of this merciless killer is amyotrophic lateral sclerosis, a mouthful challenging enough that most people know it as Lou Gehrig's disease after the baseball legend whose career was cut short by it in 1939. The body's motor neurons mysteriously die out. Motor neurons are the nerve cells that connect the brain to the spinal cord, and the spinal cord to the muscles, to give us the ability to control our voluntary muscles.

Without them our hearts still beat, our guts still digest food, but our ability to move everything else gradually peters out. That includes the diaphragm, the muscle we use to pull air into our lungs. When that one goes, you either pump air in or you die.

There is no cure. One hundred thirty-eight years after a French physician named Jean-Martin Charcot first identified the disease, and sixty-seven years after baseball's Iron Horse gave it his famous name, there is no effective therapy. Even after all the studies and tests, the beakers and microscopes, the discovery of DNA and the mapping of the human genome, medical science still cannot identify the cause in nine out of ten cases. The other ten percent are attributable to one of four genetic mutations. Researchers can accurately describe the many biochemical changes that occur in the body, in the cells, but they cannot agree on which change comes first. Is the pathogenesis of ALS a domino effect where one misfolded protein in one bad cell sets off a chain of events leading to the moribund state of a fully paralyzed person? Or are there multiple triggering dominos setting off multiple, interwoven chains of events?

Occasionally there is a fluke. The famous astrophysicist, Stephen Hawking, is now in his forty-fourth year of living with the disease while for just about everyone else, the life expectancy is dire: half will die within eighteen months of diagnosis, eighty percent within five years, and ninety percent within ten years. Dr. Hawking experienced the first symptoms at the age of nineteen, decades younger than the average age of onset of fifty. He survived twenty-two years before going on a ventilator, and may have gone longer but for a bout with pneumonia. Most neurologists would agree that his disease is something other than the one killing me, but with no answers to so many questions everyone just calls it ALS. No one knows why his experience has been different than mine.

"What can I do?" I asked the doctor. I asked about diet, and exercise, and inside myself I was screaming, "WHAT....CAN....I.....DO?!"

Once again I was a boy in Mrs. Witscher's classroom, knees shaking, empty-handed without pencil or paper on the first day of school. There is no substitute for preparedness. I wanted the doctor to tell me what I could do to prepare for a terminal illness. I wanted a flight for which I could pack, a meeting for which I could gather data. I had taken Mrs. Witscher's command to heart and thus far it had kept me in good standing. But now my standing literally was in question.

I drove home with my windows open and the radio blaring. "Take me away from this!" I wanted to yell to anyone within earshot. "This can't be happening to me," I thought. At home I climbed the stairs from the garage to the kitchen. Eve had come home from work while I was at the clinic, and was baking homemade bread. A loaf in the oven filled the house with a delicious aroma. The counter was covered in flour. Eve was too.

"What did they say?" she asked while kneading a second batch of raw dough.

"The doctor said he had ruled out everything but ALS." I replied flatly. Eve turned from her big bowl and hugged me with her upper arms, careful not to touch me with her powdered hands.

"When I asked him what the next step would be he told me, 'There's nothing you can do,'" I said. She didn't say anything, and after a few seconds went back to her kneading.

Nothing I can do? Nothing?!

I would not accept that. I never have. I never will.

Chapter Five

Ike

After our wedding Eve and I moved into our dream house in the Richmond district of San Francisco, tucked in the northwest corner of the city just over a rise from the Golden Gate Bridge. The house was tall, narrow, and deep, like so many others built on the San Francisco peninsula where open lots had been scarce for decades. It was built originally in 1907, the year after the great earthquake that destroyed much of the city, and though it had been renovated several times over the years, it was a fixer-upper when we bought it, in need of new everything including the kitchen sink. But when the contractor had finished hammering, painting, and polishing, the house was exactly what we wanted, all the way down to the hand-painted kitchen tiles we had bought in Italy on our honeymoon. From my home office on the top floor I had a broad view of the park just behind our back gate, and beyond into the Presidio.

Late at night, the park behind our house was silent. The bustling daytime world with its happy yaps and chirps had shut down, and although now I can see how these changes foreshadowed the shut down to come in my body, at the time I found comfort in the silence and darkness. They were maternal, welcoming, reassuring in ways I deeply needed. Eve asleep in the next room, I sat for hours hunched at my desk, tap, tap, tapping my fingers at the keyboard, as if I were undergoing a perpetual neurological exam. Which in fact I was; my legs continued to stiffen, the weakness in my left arm worsened and began in my right hand as well. Until then my diminishing strength and coordination had not interfered with my daily life, but as both hands became impaired I began to struggle with even the simplest tasks such as cutting my food. To compensate I started avoiding challenging meals. No more steak or chicken. No more long pasta which I couldn't curl onto a fork. Eve helped me by making food I could either grip with both hands, like sandwiches made in pita pockets, or stab easily with a fork, like tortellini.

Now that the doctor had given my symptoms a possible name, I went online with an insatiable hunger for information, spending all my free time scouring the Internet. Across my screen flickered medical articles, dietary regimes, and countless patient narratives from people desperately seeking solace by telling their stories to the world.

It seemed strange to think I had spent my entire life until that point taking it for granted that I could throw a ball, or tie my shoes, or butter a piece of toast, when in fact even such simple movements require elaborate communications to and from the brain, all in a fraction of a second. I had kicked stones on a beach, stepped onto a bus, walked for miles in Greece, London, Moscow – and assumed my legs could continue to walk wherever I chose. It seemed I could no longer make those assumptions. I learned that only my mind would not atrophy. I would understand every loss of muscle function as it happened.

So I made an appointment to see Dr. Jeffrey Rothstein, one of the top ALS researchers in the world and director of the ALS center at Johns Hopkins University. I did at one point ask myself why I was getting on a plane to Baltimore when every day my body showed evidence of increased spasticity and muscle weakness. Like every informed American who believes our medical establishment is second to none, I told myself I was entitled to a second opinion, and that afterwards I would have nowhere else to look for explanations. Certainly I wanted a definitive diagnosis. And yet I'll admit I traveled to Baltimore because I had allowed an infinitesimal part of myself to hope I had to consider only ALS. Or maybe I just wanted to talk to the guy.

By the time I went to see Dr. Rothstein it was July 2001, almost a year since Dr. Miller had told me to consider ALS. The morning I was to leave for Baltimore, Eve and I ate breakfast in our bright kitchen overlooking the beautiful greenery of the park, in what I had begun to think of as our "house of denial." For the house represented the normal life we once believed we could have—the mornings I would run in the park, the afternoons I would climb two flights of stairs to work in my home office, the nights I would sit in my parlor chair listening to music with my wife's little, nimble body draped on one of its wide arms.

"I'll call you when I get there," I said to Eve as we drank our glasses of orange juice. Buried deep in the lethargy I had felt since that last visit to Dr. Miller,

I didn't even think to say something more gratuitous like, "I know this has been hard on you, too." Despite how close we felt to each other then, two months after our first anniversary, our conversation rarely strayed into emotional territory even if our hearts had. Instead, my health became the topic we avoided, the elephant in the room too big to miss but too big to address.

So we sat there then in our kitchen with its fancy appliances, the morning mist drifting over the trees of the park, the foghorns of the Golden Gate Bridge blowing in the distance. Eve looked up from her cereal and smiled at me, that dazzling smile I had first fallen for in Moscow, and for a moment I felt back to our beginning, when all I had to worry about was keeping our relationship a secret. Already it seemed a long time ago; we were no longer the couple who had enjoyed Friday night concerts at the Moscow Conservatory. We were older now; less innocent. My arm had aged forty years, and I struggled to be the person I once had been.

"When I get back..." I began to say.

"I want you to do something for me," she said.

"Sure." I had been about to suggest we plan something special for ourselves, maybe a weekend up in wine country near where we'd had our wedding. I wanted to tell her I would try to keep things good for as long as I could.

"I have the name of a Reiki practitioner" she went on, "who's supposed to be really great. I want to call her and I want you to go with me."

"Eve," I sighed. "I don't have time for that." We had been through this before; Eve wanting me to try alternative health therapies that I didn't believe in, and saw as – at best – placebos.

"If I were you…" she started.

"But you're not me," I snapped. "And I'm not going to my waste my time on jokers like that. Every dollar we spend now on hocus pocus is a dollar we won't be able to spend later on life support."

I was irritated that on the very morning I was flying to see a man of science, a world expert in the proven workings of a complex, terminal disease, she was thinking about spending time and money on someone who claimed she could heal people by passing her hands an inch or so above various parts of the body. Eve's faith in alternative therapies had not arisen spontaneously. When we were still in Moscow she had experienced a minor but uncomfortable health problem that doctors could not seem to fix. One French doctor actually prescribed a particular brand of bottled water that she should drink every day. I sent one of our company drivers out to find some of it, and wondered on what planet the doctor had earned his title. As with most things that piqued Eve's curiosity, she pursued it aggressively, studying herbal remedies and self-help health guides. In a few weeks she had cured herself, and in doing so found justification for her growing sense that western medicine could not always provide answers.

Once back in the U.S., Eve began exploring alternative medicine more thoroughly. She took a job as the marketing director for a dot-com company selling natural remedies. Through a friend there she met and began consulting with an expert in Ayurveda, the ancient Indian system of diet and lifestyle designed to promote health and well-being of the mind, body, and soul. A year and a half later, by the summer of 2001, after following the strict dietary regime she had fashioned with the expert, and having intensively taken up yoga, both physically and spiritually, Eve was in great shape and she felt better than she had in years. Her experience with alternative medicine and a spiritually enriched lifestyle had given her good reasons to believe in therapies developed outside the confines of allopathic medicine. But my health issues were serious, so serious that if there had been anything useful in any field of human study, I reasoned that someone equally desperate would have found it years ago. I don't mean to suggest there is nothing useful in Ayurveda or any other alternative therapy, but that they have no miracle cure for me.

So when Eve pressed me to try various alternatives, besides feeling irritated I felt sad too, because it reminded me of a major difference between us. Eve is a person of deep spirituality. Her faith is such that there are some things she accepts without questioning, regardless of reason. But my equally deep faith, in humanity's capacity for genius, is such that I accept nothing without questioning.

In searching the Internet for information about fighting ALS I found dozens of patient-written narratives chronicling the authors' experiences. While most seemed focused on the past and present, asking why their lives had detoured to tragedy, some of them looked forward, describing dietary and vitamin regimens that the authors were following in an attempt to slow the progression of the disease. I read all of them looking for common themes in the vitamin cocktails they described, such as anti-oxidants or immune system boosters. From that I designed a regimen for myself, went to a nutritional supplements store to stock up, and began swallowing pills like a rock star.

I also asked Eve to read some of the websites I found most compelling so we could structure a new diet for me. I thought the stories might resonate for her. After all, her new Ayurvedic approach to her own dietary habits seemed to parallel the thoughts of many of the websites' authors, that your body's particular structure and condition dictate a particular regimen to follow. But between Eve's positive experience with alternative medicine and my own refusal to try therapies not based on scientific principles lay an abyss, one that only grew wider and deeper.

Alone, I flew to Baltimore. I took a cab to my hotel from the airport. When I got out of the cab I had to ask the bellhop to pull my wallet out of my back pocket to pay the fare. I was exhausted from the trip, sticky and limp from the heat. The air conditioner blasting cool air into my room, I lay down and napped, and when I woke it was about dinner time. I felt refreshed and hungry, so I went to the hotel restaurant, making sure to sit in a corner booth where nobody could stare at my bony, atrophied arms as if I were an animal in the zoo. Without Eve to cut my food, I ordered fish and a side of broccoli. When the waiter brought my meal, he set the broccoli to the side, a whole head, a lush gigantic tree looming on the plate.

'Uh-oh,' I thought. 'What should I do? If I ask him to cut it, will he think I'm an imperious jerk?' I was embarrassed. After all, who can't cut a steamed head of broccoli? And I was afraid to say the words, to say 'I have Lou Gehrig's disease,' as if saying them might make it incontrovertibly true.

"Could you do me a favor?" I asked the waiter. "My hands don't work very well, so could you chop the broccoli?" He was happy to help. At the time, my left hand was weaker than my right, but my left bicep was stronger, so although I was right-handed I had to eat with my left hand to lift the food up and into my mouth. It was a good dinner. Back in my room, I called Eve, and then lay in bed watching old movies before falling asleep again.

The next morning I took a taxi over to the medical center. In the back seat listening to the Indian music the driver had blasting out of the car's scratchy speakers I lay my hands on my thighs and flexed them, feeling the thousands of muscle strands beneath my skin vibrating because they were receiving scratchy signals from my brain. It was hot in the cab, the air-condition-ing lame, but I could not turn the handle to manually open the window. It was July 14, Bastille Day in France, a day of celebration to mark their independence. For me, of course, my independence was fading. If I'd had any question months ago, when I had made this appointment for a second opinion, by now there really was no doubt in my mind that it was ALS. I couldn't manipulate my wallet. It was difficult to haul my body out of the cab. Walking from the curb to the medical center was an ordeal. But I could sweat, and I could curse, and I could still make it to my appointment with Dr. Rothstein.

The consultation was brief. After the usual neurological exam the doctor looked at my atrophying body, and I looked at the grave expression on his face, and we both knew there was little to say. "Is there any doubt in your mind that it's ALS?" I asked. He shook his head and spoke sympathetically.

"I'm afraid I have no doubts, Jack," he said. "It's ALS." I nodded.

"I guess I just wanted to hear it from you." In the year since Dr. Miller had ruled out alternative explanations I had absorbed plenty of information about ALS. Long gone were the days when I would enter a neurologist's office without a list of questions and an appetite for discussion. "So what's the status of your research on stem cell-based therapies?" I asked. "I read on your website you've had promising results in mice." The question surprised him. Perhaps when others received an ALS diagnosis from him their minds would go blank from the shock, just as mine had a year earlier. His tone changed immediately.

"Yes, they have been promising. We knocked out the lower motor neurons in the test animals to produce total lower body paralysis. Then we injected neural stem cells, those that differentiate into the cell types of the nervous system, into their spinal fluid. Eight weeks later, half of the treated mice can plant their feet."

Wait a minute…did he just say reversal of paralysis?! Those were magic words to me, words that made hope so tangible I could feel it tickle the back of my throat. "So when will it be available for human testing?" I asked excitedly.

"If all goes well, maybe in about two years," he said. "First we need to see what happens in the ALS mouse. It's one thing to restore function in a paralyzed but stable animal. But the ALS mouse, just like humans with ALS, experiences progressive loss of function. Before we can try this sort of therapy we need to dramatically slow or stop the underlying disease process. Otherwise, any new neural tissue arising from the injected stem cells will deteriorate just like the original tissue damaged by the disease. The bottom line with this and all other stem cell-based therapies is that we can't treat people until we have a more thorough understanding of the possible risks."

It all sounded logical, of course. But when your own mortality is staring you in the face, it's tempting to disregard logic. After all, wasn't that a source of friction between Eve and me? She accepted the possibility that methods she could not explain might actually help, and I simply did not. But in that little room with a world-renowned scientist I caught a glimpse of her side of the abyss. 'Hey Doc,' I wanted to say, 'I don't need to know all the risks. Give me whatever forms I need to sign and let's go, because in two years it could be too late.'

Drowning in desperation, I thrashed about trying to find a rope to grab. His guess on the timeframe for a stem cell-based therapy left me with a string of hope the thickness of sewing thread. And though just twenty-six days later the Bush administration would announce restrictions on federal funding of embryonic stem cell research that significantly retarded that two-year timeline, I squeezed as tightly as I could.

A clump of embryonic stem cells is so small it could rest on the sharp end of a pin, yet it appears to open a new field in therapeutics, regenerative medicine. Because embryonic stem cells can develop into any of the 220 types of cells in the human body, they hold enormous potential to treat a long list of illnesses. Unfortunately, it is not as simple as injecting a batch of stem cells into the part of the body not functioning properly. Before embryonic stem cells can be used to treat those who are ill, medical science needs to know how they work.

The biochemistry of the human body is based on roughly 30,000 different proteins. Each one has a specific role in the functions we take for granted; from converting food into energy, to enabling communication between the brain and the rest of the body, to regulating the homeostatic balance of all our tissues working in concert. In addition, proteins underlie the processes by which a microscopic clump of embryonic stem cells grows and differentiates into the trillions of cells in a human adult. Before researchers can develop stem cell-based therapies they need to know how much of which proteins, in which order, and at what times to use them to coax embryonic stem cells to develop. And even when they discover the secrets of stem cell development in a fetus, they need to explore how the many developmental pathways might need to be altered to achieve the desired result in the adult body. The multitude of questions begs for intensive research.

In the narrow application of stem cell-based therapies for those with ALS, many questions about how the disease begins and progresses needed to be answered before doctors could engineer a way to regenerate motor neurons. As Dr. Rothstein had noted, the fact that ALS is a progressive disease meant that new neurons would succumb to it just as others already had done.

I had more questions for the doctor but his next appointment beckoned. A few months later I continued that conversation with Dr. John MacDonald, a neurologist then at Washington University who would become a good friend.

"Why not just inject neural stem cells repeatedly?" I asked. "Then maybe you could achieve a kind of equilibrium between neurons lost in the disease pathogenesis, and neurons gained from injected stem cells.

"Although that's an enticing idea," he answered, "it doesn't factor in the many other possible outcomes from injected stem cells. For example, what if the injected cells differentiate, not into neurons, but into tumors riddled throughout the central nervous system?"

"Well, if they become neurons in the mouse, can't you presume they'd become neurons in humans?"

"Yes and no," he said. "While we don't need to guide every developmental stage of the injected cells, we need to know we can block certain pathways, such as any that could lead to cancerous cells, before we try to treat humans with it."

"Then why not inject cells that have already begun to differentiate into neurons?"

"Well, there is evidence suggesting that the cells we really want aren't neurons after all. We've found that when neurons carrying one of the ALS genes, called SOD1, are supported by non-SOD1 astrocytes, the cells that nourish and support neurons, the neurons remain healthy. And in the reverse case, when neurons without the mutated gene are supported by astrocytes that do have it, the neuron still fails."

"So if a person with the SOD1 mutation has diseased astrocytes and neurons, how can they be treated?"

"Through gene therapy. Theoretically, we would engineer a benign virus carrying a normal SOD1 gene, and inject it into the spinal fluid. Then, just like any virus, it would seek to introduce its DNA into the patient's cells, repairing the mutation."

Conversations like this one played an important part in surviving the emotional roller-coaster I boarded when I was diagnosed with ALS. Even in tragedy, such as when Pandora, the first woman in Greek mythology, opened Epimetheus' jar to release all the plagues of mankind, hope remains.

I made it back to my hotel where I packed my bags and checked out, and then I grabbed another cab to the airport. I had to wait for my flight to St. Louis, where I would visit my parents. They knew I had consulted with neurologists but I hadn't told them my symptoms pointed to ALS because until then I hadn't been absolutely sure. I sat near the window where my flight would be called and sipped an orange juice, aware of the effort it took my throat muscles to swallow the cold liquid. I thought about Bastille Day in Paris. Exactly twelve years earlier I had stood on the Champs-Elysees with my lifelong friend, Mark Jaffe, and hundreds of thousands of others to celebrate the 200th anniversary of French republicanism. I remembered the jubilant throngs dancing in the streets, the musicians playing for passers-by with their hats on the sidewalk full of coins, and the children gorging on candy with balloons tied to their wrists. I imagined the City of Lights at night, its avenues flooded by street-lamps and its white stone embankments along the Seine that shone in the dark. I imagined night falling and the fireworks going off and I remembered how spectacular fireworks always seemed to me as a child, craning my neck back as far as it could go. What else can a firework be but lovely as it breaks into flame above? Not now, not for me. What I see is a black background, a bang, a scatter of blue cells. They form a flower in the sky, stay for a second, and then fall fast.

In St. Louis, my Dad and I sat in the library of the house in which I grew up, and watched the evening news. It was a familiar scene, one replayed hundreds of times from when I was a child still living at home and then as an adult come to visit. Over the years, the television screen had grown larger, the couch had been replaced, and Dan Rather had aged, but the essential elements had not changed. I sat buried in an over-stuffed chair. My Dad sat low on the adjacent couch with his feet up. At age eighty, he had a bad heart, weak legs from polio sixty-five years earlier, a hodgepodge of early-stage skin cancers, an enlarging prostate, ears damaged by the guns of the destroyer escort on which he had spent most of World War II, arthritic joints, and hypothyroidism. Meanwhile I was supposed to be young and healthy, decades further from death than he. I had worried about my Dad's health for years, his descent during my ascent. But now my body had changed in ways I never expected. The cushy chair was no longer as comfortable for me. I hoped my Dad wouldn't notice that I let him work the remote control. But more than that, my vision had changed. This room in which I had spent thousands of hours now seemed strangely precious and surprisingly strange. How quickly a thing passes and becomes something else, I thought. How fragile are the tethers that bind us to normality, or even reality; for now, instead of fearing my Dad's heart would give out I felt a glimmer of a wish that he might die before I did. I had heard that the most wrenching experience for a parent is to lose a child, and I dreaded having to tell my Dad about my diagnosis.

But during a break in the news he asked if the doctors had anything to say about my condition. I may not have told my parents my secrets throughout my life but I would not lie. "He said he had no other explanation than Lou Gehrig's disease," I said.

"Oh, no," was all he said. I watched my Dad's face turn gray, and then slacken with sadness. And then he put his weathered hand on mine and I felt sad, too, but reassured also by the warmth of his touch.

Later that night, when my Mom came home, she walked into my room and got right to the point. "I heard you saw a neurologist in Baltimore. And although I know you're trying to protect us, we're still your parents and have a right to know about you."

I had wanted so badly to keep them sheltered from my nightmare. My Mom had just been diagnosed with stage three lung cancer, and I'd had the crazy idea that she, too, would die before I did. Now that was over. I had to come clean. "He said it's ALS, that it's a relatively slow progression, that stem cell research will probably be a reasonable therapy in about two years, and that I should go on living my life without worrying about it because the statistics suggest I'll outlive you and Dad."

If I had expected drama or tears it was only because I had forgotten how strong my Mom is during adversity. She had survived the death of her first husband, the near death of my Dad several times, and the deaths of plenty of her friends from old age and infirmity. She responded to my news calmly and pragmatically. "You'll have to do the best you can," she said. "Keep up with the research, I know you will."

As painful as it was to have to share the news with my parents, it was also a relief not to have to hide my illness from them anymore, and to see that they had not been crushed by the awful truth. I felt less burdened knowing they would share some of the worry now. Even so, I didn't invite them to share every detail of my deterioration, every whim how to fight it. As in my personal life, where I had erected carefully placed borders to protect my privacy and independence, I did the same with my health. Why share all the nattering noise of my personal nightmare with them,

and force them to endure it with me, when I could protect and insulate them? Doesn't a dutiful son do that
for his parents?

Alone again in my boyhood room, I allowed
myself to indulge my emotions, to wallow in self-pity,
something I had been doing a lot of in the past year. I
didn't go out for the rest of my visit. I hid from my
old friends, didn't even want to talk to them on the
phone. Anyone who has ever been diagnosed with a
serious illness, let alone a terminal one, has every right
to feel miserable. You're mourning who you could
have been but never will be. You're coming to terms
with the future, the dreams you've lost. And you're
giving up the expectation you once had for a normal
and long life.

From St. Louis I was to fly back to San Francisco, and my parents took me to the airport. They
stood at the gate to see me off. This, too, was a familiar scene, one that had been repeated countless times,
first when I went to Europe on the guided student trips
of my teenage summers, then when I went to college,
then to Europe, then to Russia. Always I am in a plane
and my parents are two tiny figures far from me, waving as the engines start, and always I am waving back,
goodbye. And always before I was afraid that this was
to be the last farewell we would be lucky enough to
have, because my Dad's heart, his poor pump, might
give out. In college I'd had recurring nightmares of
his death; I lived through my young adult years with
an imagined but persistent background noise, the en-
gine of his heart. But now, as I waved to my Dad I realized that, perhaps, he was waving to me. The roles

were reversed, he was bidding me farewell and my great sadness was not that I was rising toward the sky, but that he was there, on earth, watching me as I moved on.

Back in California, I kept my promise to Eve to visit the Reiki healer she asked me to try. On a chilly night we drove south of Oakland to her home. We didn't say much on the way. Earlier, we had fought, me saying the therapy was unproven, pure nonsense, and she saying I should be more open-minded. Lately, Eve had been pushing other alternative therapies she wanted me to try, her Ayurvedic consultant, a chi-gung instructor. Finally, I gave in to her point of view, figuring the worst that could happen was that I would waste a few hours and a couple of bucks.

As we sped east over the Bay Bridge and south toward the Reiki healer's home I remember thinking that someone who claims to be able to heal others, and who has results to back it up, should have a long line of sick people standing around waiting their turn. But when we arrived, the house was dark and quiet. The healer answered the doorbell and led us into a small room that had a massage table and a credenza covered with vials containing various flower oils. I resisted the urge to say something cutting. The healer asked me to lie on the table on my back and try to relax. She dimmed the lights and lit an aromatic candle. Eve took a chair and sat quietly in the corner.

The healer placed her hands about an inch or two above my body and slowly began to move them over my arms, legs, abdomen, chest and head. As she moved over various parts of my body she described what those parts were calling out for. "Your chest is calling for love and acceptance. Your head needs the true knowledge that is wisdom." I was almost enjoying the show as a kind of mock theater when she announced with great certainty, "Your arms desperately want to be one with God." I bit down on the inside of my mouth, trying not to laugh.

During the ride home, tension hung thick as Spanish moss, obscuring our view of each other. "Did you really pay that woman $120?" I asked.

"Yes, I did," said Eve, who sat in the passenger seat looking out the window to her right, avoiding catching my eye.

"I can respect acupuncture as a scientific discipline, even Ayurveda as a dietary regimen developed through thousands of years of trial and error, but that was a joke." The theatrical entertainment value of the evening had passed. Now I was just irritated. I tried to think of it as money spent on our marriage, not on a fraud.

Eve wouldn't look at me. I'm sure she knew we had been taken, but she didn't want to say so for fear that it might represent an admission that all alternative therapies were a hoax. Who was fooling whom? We both knew neither one of us was happy about what had just happened. The Reiki healer had magically lifted $120 out of our bank account, and pulled out the first of the stitches holding our marriage together.

After Dr. Miller had given his preliminary diagnosis a year earlier, I never saw him again. In three follow-up appointments at his clinic, he left me to his neurology residents, a pair of young Russian émigrés. Although it helped dampen my anxiety to chat in Russian with them about their former homeland, it also greatly irritated me that I no longer merited a face-to-face conversation with Dr. Miller. So after his third absence, I booked an appointment at the other ALS clinic in San Francisco, the one founded by the now famous Dr. Rick Olney at the University of California San Francisco Medical Center. Also a nationally recognized leader in ALS clinical research, he had a reputation for spending a lot of time talking with his patients. Before he had devoted his career to ALS, Dr. Olney had trained as a psychiatrist, and I had heard him say his background helped him counsel patients about their fears and talk to them about death.

By the date of my first visit to his clinic I had dug through mountains of ALS research papers. I had read that high doses of Celebrex, an anti-inflammatory medication usually used to treat arthritis, could retard the progression of ALS. I had tried to bring this up with Dr. Miller, but he refused to even consider writing me a prescription. He had one of his staff return my call who could only relay his refusal.

"Dr. Olney," I said frankly, "I'm here because I want a doctor willing to work with me, to let me experiment as long as there aren't overwhelming safety issues."

He looked at me, and for once I didn't feel fragmented or collapsed, a mere compendium of failed motor neurons and weakening body parts. He saw through all that to something essential. "If I could cure you, I'd give you a regimen and expect you to follow it," he said simply. "But I can't."

"I know that," I said.

In most illnesses, even fatal ones, we expect our specialists to offer us hope in the form of a regimen or treatment. No matter how painful the treatment might be or how slim the odds are that it will make us better, we expect a doctor to give us something to try. But with ALS this helplessness, the inability to offer even a shot at a cure is almost as heartbreaking for the doctor as for the patient. Almost. They didn't go into medicine to hand out death sentences. The good ones among them will admit they don't have all the answers, and the best will admit that some of what they think they know is probably wrong, especially in neurology. Dr. Olney's approach, his willingness to experiment in partnership with his patients, made me feel less helpless.

"I'd like to try Celebrex," I said.

"No problem," he replied. "There are good reasons to think it might slow the progression. And beyond anti-inflammatory medications, if you can demonstrate that a drug might be expected to extend ALS longevity, and has been through human clinical trials even for other health issues," he said soothingly, "then I'm willing to read the literature and structure a protocol with you. Have you heard about Ritonavir?"

I left Dr. Olney's office that day feeling immensely relieved and grateful. Finally, I had found someone with an open mind and equal doses of intelligence, common sense, and compassion. I went to see him every three months, and never again suffered the anxiety that had overtaken me in Dr. Miller's office. Perhaps because neither Dr. Olney nor I expected I could be cured we focused our attention elsewhere. Certainly, we addressed how to extend my life, but we also focused on improving the time I had left through speech, occupational, and physical therapy. The rapport Dr. Olney and I developed allowed me to access untapped reservoirs of inner strength, to focus on living with ALS, not dying from it.

Ultimately, I did not stay in San Francisco so I had no idea of Dr. Olney's fate, and learned of it only later. His first symptoms appeared in 2004, after I had moved to St. Louis. After undergoing back surgery to address a compressed disk, which did nothing to alleviate the twitching in his legs, it became obvious that the ALS specialist had ALS. Then he had to face the same awful truth he had spent an entire career fighting on behalf of his patients.

Shortly before getting sick, Dr. Olney had designed an ambitious clinical trial testing to determine if two drugs used to treat AIDS and cancer might also help some ALS patients. It was to be a double-blind study, meaning that some of the participants would receive the AIDS drug, a protease inhibitor called Ritonavir, some would receive the cancer drug, and some would receive a placebo. Neither patients nor the doctors administrating the drugs would know who was receiving what.

What made headlines, in part, was that Dr. Olney made a point to be the first patient to sign up for the clinical trial. Given his position, he could easily have taken one of the drugs, or both of them, for that matter. He could have bypassed the protocols and, with them, the chance of receiving the placebo. But he didn't. His altruism – to choose to go into a trial on behalf of patients who would come after him – has made him a powerful hero to many in the ALS community.

In late 2000, when I still struggled with my preliminary diagnosis, I finally agreed to get a dog. Eve had wanted one for ages, and now, anticipating my shortened lifespan, I saw that I should not postpone any future plans, even small ones such as getting a dog. And I thought a dog would offer comfort to Eve, and to me, too. If nothing else, we needed a distraction.

As a child Eve had begged her parents for years before they finally gave her a Llasa Apso on her tenth birthday, so she was partial to smaller, long-haired dogs. But I didn't want a little, yippee thing. In fact, the more we looked at various websites, the more I knew exactly what I wanted in a dog. I developed a long list of traits, something for which Eve would later tease me.

"How about a Tibetan Terrier?" she suggested.

"Nah, too hairy," I replied. "We'll have to bathe it after every romp at the dog run."

"What about a Bernese mountain dog like the one we saw in the park?" she asked.

"Now that was a gorgeous dog. I read they have a really short lifespan, like six to eight years."

"Oh, then that's not a good idea," she said. 'Why not?' I thought. Is longevity a prerequisite for happiness? Surely, a dog wouldn't understand any part of this idea. He lives entirely in the present, unaware of himself, fully occupied by base instincts and desire – for food, for play, for affection. Our self-awareness gives us an understanding of our past and future, and the ability to hope. To pity a dog with a life expectancy half as long as most other dogs is to project our own fear of death onto him.

"How about a lab?" Eve offered.

"Nah, they're really hyper the first few years so you have to walk them a lot."

"Well, you'll be here to walk a dog any time he wants."

The words were barely out of her mouth when I thought, "I'm not so sure about that." But I didn't want to darken a nice conversation, so I said, "Well, can walking be your job, and I'll take care of training?"

"I'm not doing all the walking," she said. "You're going to have to help." I'm sure she didn't have a subtext in mind but I felt one. As I started to accept the fact that I might have ALS, it seemed like every conversation, not just with Eve but with anyone, crossed into questionable territory, the future. I had always been an optimist, but my deteriorating health was changing even my nature. "There's no doubt about it," I thought. "I'm losing my identity too."

So it went for a week or two, both of us excited at the thought of getting a dog, and pleased to have a subject in which to get immersed. In looking for a dog we felt occupied and utterly in control, a pleasant change from contemplating my helplessness and hopelessness every day. Yet reading about the temperament for each breed was unsettling for me. Unlike human beings, dogs can be bred for specific traits – sociability or shyness, aggressive behavior or calm friendliness, protectiveness, loyalty, independence. I liked being able to choose the personality of the creature who'd be living with us, but even so, I was struck by how much control we assume we have. I thought back to Father Mendel, to his carefully cultivated pea plants, how he watered them each day and watched them grow, discovering that the larger leaf or the greener pea was an inherited trait. I thought about supermarket peaches that no longer had fuzz, and fat, juicy heirloom tomatoes that don't go soft for a week. Was this passion for genetic control right or wrong? Or perhaps the moral framework we use to consider such issues is somehow the wrong one for the question?

And then my thoughts turned to the contemporary genome project, to the progress made in identifying the specific genes that cause inherited illnesses and the futuristic dream of being able to turn off the genes we don't want and turn on the ones we do. Will the future of genomics make it possible to design children before they are born? Surely, if modern medicine could eliminate deadly inherited disorders such as cystic fibrosis or type-1 diabetes, few would argue against it. But what about genetic traits that our culture simply prefers, such as blonde hair, or blue eyes, or a slim physique? Where should we stop tinkering with our genetic constitution and just accept our differences? Thus far, my disease cannot be traced to a genetic mutation, so doctors call it "sporadic," seemingly isolated and thus impossible to predict. We can't breed for or against ALS in the human species.

A few days into my puppy finding mission I was skimming through a book about dogs Eve had bought. With weakened hands I couldn't hold the pages of the book to turn them, and even if I could have grabbed them my arms and shoulders would have gotten worn out from lifting them repeatedly off my lap. So each time I needed to turn a page I'd stand up, brush my hand hanging at my side across the page, and sit back down. Flipping through the dog book, that's when I saw it – the Entlebucher Mountain Dog. He was medium-sized, tri-colored with a medium-thick shiny coat, had floppy ears, was highly intelligent, calm but needing plenty of exercise, protective ever since his ancestor's days as a cattle herder, and a loyal and loving family member. In other words, perfect.

"EEEEEEEVE!!" I shouted.

We found a list of breeders online and started calling around to see if any of them had pups available. Since my speech had started to slur we decided Eve should make the calls. Human sounds are produced in the larynx, and until I had begun my frenzied ALS research, I hadn't realized that the larynx is made up of four kinds of muscles; deep folds of muscles that are necessary to carry the voice. As those muscles weakened I began to sound hoarse all the time, and I had trouble speaking loudly. I hid it as well as I could, but I was terrified about losing my voice. I registered with a research laboratory in Delaware that had developed software to recreate your voice through a computer. I followed the set up procedure, recording over 1,600 phrases that the software chopped up into every syllable and consonant-vowel combination used in the English language. Then, reordering those bits to form whatever I want to say, it would spit out a slightly choppy and monotonous voice. But it was my voice.

"Yes, yes," Eve assured a breeder who was interviewing her. "Right behind our house is a park with a dog run. He'd have plenty of exercise. Plenty of dog company, too. It's a very popular spot with dog owners."

"Will you have time to spend with the dog? This particular breed is very social." The breeder sounded suspicious. I wondered if she was like that with every caller.

"My husband works at home. He can take a break, you know, to play with the dog." All the breeders had an extensive questionnaire we had to answer satisfactorily to be an approved puppy owner, but no one asked, "Do you have Lou Gehrig's Disease?"

'I'm still here, still here like always,' I wanted to say. The more I lost of my original self, the more defensive I became of the person I had been. It raised many deep, philosophical questions. What is the self? Is it what I do, or what I can do? Is it what I say, or what I think? If it's all of these to some degree, then am I less myself, less of a person, when I lose some of these dimensions? Beyond the challenge to my identity, the loss of my original self forced me to hold even more tightly to the scraps still remaining, the things I could still do, and my general sense of hopefulness, that tomorrow could always be better than today.

Some people experience the progression of ALS as a set of slopes and plateaus. They decline for awhile, and then stabilize for awhile. Others, including myself, decline steadily, continually losing strength and coordination. For most people, the loss of function is not discernable daily or even weekly, but over a month the changes become apparent. At first you can no longer hold a cup steady to drink from, and then you can no longer drink from a straw, and then, at last, you can no longer drink at all.

In 2000, as more of my musculature fell prey to the disease, I became hyper-aware of every miniscule change in my strength and coordination. As I walked around the house or the neighborhood I would test my legs with each step – drag this toe without stubbing it, slide that heel without dropping those toes, climb stairs two at a time to see if it feels different than I remember. With the disease taking a little more each day, I struggled to keep believing tomorrow could be better than today.

It took a few weeks to mail papers back and forth with the breeder, but on January 5, 2001, Eve and I went to the airport to meet our new puppy. He arrived in a crate, and at first when we opened the crate door he lay still, frightened by his eight-hour journey and this new, noisy place. I hadn't anticipated this raw terror and I suddenly felt it was cruel to transport a six-month old puppy like that. Didn't I know that terror, too, of finding yourself in unfamiliar surroundings with no ability to return to where you feel comfortable? The only difference was that I could hide it better. Eve spoke sweetly to him to coax him out of the crate. When he emerged Eve clipped a leash on him and led him out of the baggage claim area to pee. I couldn't lift the crate so I dragged it out to our car where Eve was waiting with our disoriented pooch.

We played with the dog non-stop for the first two days. I couldn't grip a tennis ball to throw it for him but I kicked one around the kitchen. He ran for it, ears flapping, legs moving too quickly in excitement, front paws sliding out from under him as he slipped on the hardwood floor, picked himself up and lunged forward. We laughed at his antics. 'What a spaz,' I thought. And then I filled with grief because looking at his rounded, muscular form I knew he would grow out of his spasticity. For him it added to his cuteness, especially because soon he would lose it as he matured into a graceful, athletic animal. But for me spasticity meant degradation.

The dog, whom we named Ike, became my first portal to grief. I felt self-pitying in those days, but sitting alone at home I had no outlet for it. I got into the habit of taking Ike for a walk around lunchtime. I would barely get out the door in our back fence before the tears would start pouring down my face, tears I didn't want to show to Eve or my family or friends. During the hour walk I would get it out of my system by crying and talking to Ike, who listened carefully as long as I continued to kick his slobbery tennis ball.

But that first day, watching Ike's "spasticity," I wasn't ready for the grief percolating inside me. His beautiful form and fluid motions made him fascinating to watch but they sparked jealousy in me. I wanted so much to share his ease and gracefulness. How much of his actions were learned and how much were instinctive? How did he know to crouch with his front legs extended out and his rear end in the air to signal that he wanted to play? And why, at about nine months old, did he switch from squatting when he had to pee to lifting a back leg? Did he learn these movements from watching other dogs?

After returning from our walks I too had to pee. Ike would follow me into the bathroom where I struggled to unzip my pants. Even after I attached little metal rings to the zippers of all my pants, it was always a race to get my clumsy fingers in the ring and pull down before I could not hold it any longer. Like a little boy who doesn't want to stop playing to relieve himself, I would dance around trying to diminish the urge to pee long enough to get a finger through the zipper ring and pull down. I wondered if Ike would learn to dance too before heeding nature's call. Though ultimately inconsequential, obstacles like this began to loom large in my world – buttons that seemed the size of tractor tires, door knobs suspiciously bright and slippery – all objects wrong, either mocking or menacing in their ordinariness.

The first night with Ike we tried to make him sleep in the kitchen where we could clean up a puddle of pee easily, but he whined, scratched at the door, and barked. Eventually we let him come up to our bedroom where he rolled himself into a ball at the foot of the bed and fell fast asleep. All he wanted was to be close to mama. All that day and the next he followed Eve from room to room, always by her side, licking her face if she crouched to open a cabinet, bumping into the side of her leg, wagging his tail, and generally demanding constant attention. Basically, he wanted to be at her side every waking hour and then sleep beside her at night. At first she was thrilled; she had wanted a dog for a long time and enjoyed Ike's frisky affection, but after awhile she began to get irritated.

"This isn't what I imagined it would be like," she said. "It's impossible to do anything with Ike glued to my side."

Ike had been trailing Eve for something like fifty hours straight when she tried to close the bathroom door for a moment's peace, but the puppy was too fast—he wiggled past her and plopped down on the small rug in front of the shower.

"No, Ikey, please," Eve begged. "Jack! Will you come get him?"

There was something in her voice I hadn't heard before, the sound of being overwhelmed.

"Come here, Ike," I said in as stern a voice as I could muster. But he didn't move. He just lay there looking at me with his big brown eyes. I tried a sweet voice, "Come here, little Ikeypoo." But the puppy just wagged his tail and moved closer to Eve. She took a step back then, away from me, and her eyes had a vacant look as if she could just keep on stepping back and back, away and away.

"I can't take this anymore," she said.

"Can't take what?" I asked.

"Ike," she muttered. "I can't take Ike. I need to be alone for a little while."

Had she been about to say "Jack" instead of "Ike?" I tried to give Eve a break from our demanding pup. I clipped on Ike's leash and headed out to the corner grocer to pick up a few things. When I got there I realized I couldn't take a dog inside. So I tied him to a pole on the sidewalk and went in to get the groceries. As I stood at the checkout counter just fifteen feet away from him, suddenly, he pulled at the leash. It unraveled easily—I hadn't tied it securely because I would not have been able to untie it – and he dashed into the street.

The traffic light was red at the intersection just outside the store entrance. As Ike dashed, the light changed, and the first car through the intersection was a police car. Ike had never seen a car before he arrived in San Francisco, so he didn't know to be frightened of one. The police car smacked into Ike on his left side and sent him tumbling. He yelped violently, and when he stopped tumbling he kept running, across the next three lanes. I dropped everything and ran after him. Traffic had stopped completely as the policeman got out of his car. Ike was hurt and limping now, moving slowly enough so that I could catch him. But as soon as I grabbed the leash, he pulled out of his collar and scurried into an open garage where a man was cleaning out old boxes.

I ran over to the garage and asked the guy for help. By that point the policeman too had joined in the confusion. I was able to get a hand on Ike but with my weak arms I couldn't move him. "Pick up the damn dog and get out of there," shouted the policeman.

"I have Lou Gehrig's disease," I shouted back. "My arms don't work."

The policeman stormed over, grabbed Ike by the scruff of his neck and me by the arm, and dragged us both out to the sidewalk. He stuffed Ike back into his collar and wrapped the leash tightly around my wrist.

"Give the guy a break," said the homeowner from his garage.

"You pipe down," the policeman retorted. Then he turned toward me. "And you, if you don't want to lose that dog, you keep the damn leash in your hand."

Ike's blood oozed out of a gash on one of his front legs, and he cried desperately. "Officer, please help me!" I shouted at him. "My arms don't work very well. I can't get the dog home like this. Please just take me home – it's only a block from here – and I'll get my wife."

He helped me into his patrol car, placed Ike on my lap, and drove us home. I kicked at the front door until Eve answered. She was shocked at the sight of blood all over my shirt and pants. When I explained what had happened she loaded us into her car and raced to a nearby animal hospital.

At the hospital, the vet sedated Ike and examined him. I sat in the waiting area limp as overcooked linguini. And I was crying my eyes out. I didn't know if I was crying harder because of Ike, who would come out of the ordeal with a cast and a chronically arthritic elbow; or because of my arms, so damaged that I couldn't pick up my scared puppy; or because I had caught a frightening view of my future, when my disabilities would strip me of my independence, my dignity, my identity, and my life.

Chapter Six

Arc from a Springboard

♦♦♦♦♦♦♦

If you stick with a poker face, you can get by with a pair of threes, but if you curl your lip when your threes could beat your opponent's hand full of garbage, he can convince you he's holding a flush. It's better just to keep everyone guessing. At least, so I thought. I have always been a private person, never volunteering my feelings for fear they might reveal vulnerability. Until my diagnosis with ALS, I thought I could figure out how to fix whatever might be broken in my life myself. But not anymore. As the disease took hold of my hands it also dissolved away my privacy. My ever-growing need to rely on people, especially Eve, to do the small but necessary tasks of everyday life – buttoning shirts, zipping pants, cutting food, scratching my nose – constituted an all-out assault on my very identity. I tried to keep my reliance on her a secret. The very fact of it threatened my dignity.

One morning in March 2001, I woke alone in a hotel in Minneapolis. I had flown in the previous evening from San Francisco; later, I would have a meeting. But that morning, when I began to get ready, I suddenly realized that I could not button my shirt. At home, I typically worked in a t-shirt, and in St. Louis I stayed at my parents' home so I could always get my Mom to help me. But in Minneapolis I would have to ask someone for help or wait in my room for an hour or two until Connie arrived. And I was hungry. I had no choice but to put on my clothes as best I could manage. I buttoned the bottom three buttons, the ones I could reach without bending my elbows. Then I tucked the bottom of the shirt into my pants and set out for the breakfast room. As I walked down the hotel hallway I imagined the conversation I might have with the hostess.

"Hi," I would say in my most jaunty voice. "I have a disease you've probably never heard of and I can't button up my shirt, so could you help me? No, it's not contagious. No, this isn't an odd pickup line, but you do have a nice smile. No, I didn't forget my big gold chain. Yes, I know I look like I'm in good shape, but I promise I'm thoroughly screwed up. Uh, table for one please."

I turned the corner into the restaurant and felt my face flush, the adrenaline coursing through me. How had I become so easily intimidated? And let's be clear; I had intimidated myself. I had no evidence that other people felt weird about helping me. By the time I reached the hostess, I decided to say I had multiple sclerosis, since it's a disease more people are familiar with than ALS. "Hi, can I ask you a favor," I said. "I have MS and some days I just can't get all these damned buttons."

"Of course," she said without hesitation. "All the way up? I could do a tie too."

"No thanks, I gave up ties when I took up bodybuilding," I said.

The hostess chuckled. I was five foot eleven and weighed one hundred fifty-five pounds. No body builder, but no weakling, either. In retrospect I see there was no need for me to feel as embarrassed as I did. Needing is not the same as neediness but I wouldn't understand the distinction until later.

Despite losing the normal use of my arms, most people who saw me then would not have noticed anything strange about my appearance. But I grew terribly self-conscious. I would wear long-sleeved shirts every day no matter the weather to hide my skinny arms, and I kept my hands buried in my pants' pockets so they wouldn't hang limply at my sides. Meeting new people became agonizing because I would have to shake hands. My right bicep had become unstable enough that if I stuck out my hand to greet someone it would tremble noticeably as I strained against gravity. So I would wait for the other person to extend his hand first and then I would swing my torso a little to throw my hand over into his grip. Sometimes I would hit the target squarely, making it feel for him like a hearty hail-fellow-well-met handshake. Sometimes I would miss, making it seem as if I were mocking him, and I would have to make up an excuse like, 'I have some nerve damage in my arm,' and then try again red-faced.

As embarrassed as I felt with strangers, I felt much worse with friends because they knew the old Jack well enough that they would notice even the small changes I had experienced. But I was not able to confront that, not yet, so I would squirm out of invitations to dinner or to share a beer and catch up. One night a group of close friends invited Eve and me to go out for sushi. I love sushi and they knew it. I couldn't avoid it. At the restaurant I sat at the far end of our long, narrow table and practiced using chopsticks under the table. My right thumb was by then almost motionless so I couldn't manipulate the chopsticks at all in that hand. In my left hand I could keep a tight grip on them for a second or two, but then my fingers would tremble. So if I were going to reach over to the big plate of sushi and sashimi in the middle of the table I would have to grab a piece and pull back quickly. On my first shot I missed the tuna roll but one of the chopsticks stabbed through it, and as I withdrew my arm my prey came with me skewered indelicately on one chopstick. Did they notice? I looked around but they were all consumed in conversation. Would they notice if I were unusually quiet all through dinner? I knew I couldn't talk and stab sushi rolls at the same time without betraying my secret.

Feeling so self-conscious around others, I found it hard to enjoy myself outside the comfortable seclusion of my home. The world had changed for me. Trees, houses, people, all seemed somehow dumbed down, flattened and cartoonish. There were days when I really didn't want to get out of my bathrobe.

One of the few people I could talk to at that point was my sister Connie. Although we didn't have much room to find common ground as kids due to the six years' age difference between us, as adults we have grown closer, able to talk about the serious parts of our lives. I respect her judgment; I admire her intelligence and compassion. Connie was one of the people in whom I had already confided my suspicions about having ALS, and when the time came one of the first to whom I told my diagnosis.

In mid-2000, as Dr. Miller was ruling out alternative diagnoses for me, I was consulting for Pulitzer and working closely with Connie. I suppose it was only natural that as she concluded they would never invest as aggressively in "new media" as she thought they must do, and that she should leave them to pursue her own ideas, we would plan to build a new business together. Working towards a goal is what keeps me sane. Relaxation, for me, means finding and pursuing a different goal than the one on which I spend most of my time. And now, when I needed a major distraction from health issues I just wasn't ready to face, creating iSpringboard seemed like an excellent plan, one Connie and I hoped would launch a lucrative and promising business.

In the beginning, I had no reason to think I wouldn't be able to build and manage a fund with a term of ten years. Despite my fears at that point, I had no definitive diagnosis. Ten years still seemed like a short time to me. But for iSpringboard to work, we would have to race to build it. Connie and her family depended on her income, so even if Eve and I could survive several years on the money I had earned and saved, we could not waste any time. We guessed it would take at least six months before we would start generating any income. First, we needed to sign up a handful of small, early-stage companies as clients, companies that could benefit from, and would pay for, our experience and professional relationships, and in which we could invest in the future. Then we needed to find a handful of wealthy investors to commit to placing a significant sum of money at our discretion, money we would invest in our clients. To convince them, we would have to know the field we were targeting for investment extremely well. We would have to demonstrate previous success there, and persuade them to back us. It was a challenge, but one I sorely needed.

Once we began working to build the iSpringboard fund, I started to feel lighter, energized, and focused. If I felt weighed down or lethargic I would just remind myself how satisfying it would be if Connie and her family would be the beneficiaries of my efforts. Not that she needed me to build a future for herself and her family; she's extremely gifted and has a long history of success. In fact, in our new venture I was just the finance guy who could tell a good story with spreadsheets; she was the one whose judgment and experience interested the investors. But diving into work that would ultimately benefit Connie and her family was an important step for me in determining the way I would eventually redefine my life.

For a few months, my work on iSpringboard seemed to keep me feeling lighter and energetic. But the equilibrium I had found was extremely fragile. On another visit to Minneapolis, my wits fractured from the lightest touch during a day of meetings with the management team of a small software company. Connie and I had developed a nice rapport with them, and hoped we could develop a long-term relationship. We met with them in their offices, and after a full morning of discussing various ways to attract new investments, we broke for lunch. The CEO left the room to order sandwiches. That's when the company's head of sales stood up and grabbed a Nerf football I had noticed him kneading all morning. I sat cattycorner across the room from him, perhaps twenty feet away, and was the obvious receiver for this Tuesday morning quarterback.

"Hey Jack," he called. "You're in the end zone. Catch!" He tossed the ball at me. It flew to exactly where my hands would have been had I been able to raise them to catch it. But my motor skills had already left me by then. In my mind I had more than enough time to score the touchdown, but the motor neurons feeding the muscles in my arms passed the signals to catch the ball so slowly that my arms did not move. If you throw an object at a healthy person they will react – either to catch it or duck out of the way. But I didn't flinch. I could have been the side of a barn. The ball bounced away under the table.

Before anyone had time to process what had happened Connie jumped up from her seat. "He sucks at sports," she said. "Grab the ball and hit me. I'm open in the end zone!"

Actually I had been a captain of my high school football team, a linebacker who had intercepted plenty of passes intended for the other team. Connie, however, has never cared about or participated in sports. Her game is cerebral, not physical. Her ploy worked, though, because the sales guy ducked under the table to retrieve the ball, and tossed it back and forth with her a few times.

The incident left me shaken for the rest of the meeting, wondering if the guys could tell something was wrong with me. Had I asked for a straw with my drink a little too intently? Besides, who ever heard of a grown up who always drinks from a straw? I watched the CEO and the sales guy as I sipped my ice water through a straw – I could no longer control my hands well enough to hold the glass steady. No one said anything about my having missed the ball, but I wondered whether their confidence in me had been damaged. My own confidence had certainly eroded. As we left the software company's offices a short time later, Connie smiled and whispered to me, "Close one, huh?" What if she hadn't been there?

At home, I wanted Eve to cover for me, too. She did cover for me, buttoning my shirts, preparing my food, but she also suggested I go to her Ayurvedic practitioner. "No way," I would say. "Not gonna happen." I would shake my head, a little sad that her alternative way of thinking about illness was diametrically opposed to my rational, scientific approach. I wanted her to use her formidable intellect to analyze my situation with me, and to decide with me what to do. That had been the basis of the new relationship we had fashioned that evening in my car outside her apartment in San Francisco. We said we wanted to be partners in life. Yet now, trying to determine how to address the deterioration of my health, our partnership cracked. It made me feel very much alone.

I did agree to try chi-gung, a variant on tai chi, the Chinese practice of poses and motions designed to influence one's chi, or life energy. I missed going to the gym, missed that aching feeling in my muscles as I lifted weights, and figured moving and stretching would feel good regardless of whether I believed in the conceptions of chi-gung. Eve found a chi-gung instructor, a stereotypical northern Californian granola boy of about twenty-five who had a shaggy ponytail and a quiet, peaceful manner. He came to our house every week to lead us through exercises; I was supposed to practice them every day on my own. In our rear garden, the three of us began each session with a series of ritualistic stretches of the legs and torso. Next we did a lot of repetitive motions of the arms and legs that reminded me of old Bruce Lee movies. The activity seemed to calm even rambunctious Ike. Instead of begging for a romp in the dog run just a few yards away, he napped under our beautiful, flowering camellia tree, his floppy ears twitching from time to time in his sleep.

After about six months of working with Connie on iSpringboard, it was no longer a question of missed Nerf balls and sipping through straws. Although I could type well enough to e-mail clients, I could no longer hold a pen. Now my goals changed; I hoped to help set up some preliminary investment commitments and then find another finance guy to take my place. Even if I was too weak to keep working on iSpringboard, Connie could still make it work. I wanted her to make a bundle of money, to build the dream home she and her husband had planned after years of saving.

Despite the difference in our ages, Connie and I have always had a strong bond. When I was about three years old, she and I were together in the garage at our home, and she held me up to the windows so I could see the first snow. It was dark outside, but we watched the big flakes glisten as they drifted quietly past the outdoor light fastened above the garage door. And now, too, she was trying to hold me up as long as she could; both of us trying to keep our eyes on what glistened under the light rather than on the darkness that enveloped me.

Eventually, even Connie and I couldn't continue denying to ourselves that I was OK. I remember another iSpringboard meeting, this time in Kansas City. We had a half hour or so between meetings, and Connie said, "Let's duck into a store."

"What happened to the shopping moratorium?" I said. She made a face. My sister is almost as dedicated a shopper as she is a new media expert. We started up one of the long stairwells in the Kansas City Plaza. I was in front, and when I turned to tell her something that had just occurred to me about our next meeting, the toe of my shoe caught the lip of the next step. I fell forward, but because my arms were so weak, I couldn't brace my fall. My head and chest slammed down on the stair, my arms flapping down uselessly at my sides.

"Jack, Jack, are you OK?" Connie asked as she raced up to help me stand. She brushed the dirt off my clothes and checked my head where it had hit the cement. Our eyes met. I was unhurt physically, but it was a frightening moment. I looked into Connie's face and saw terror. I knew then that I could no longer continue denying how debilitating my disease was. I could no longer pretend that I could be her finance guy. I had leapt all right, leapt forwards and downwards, and landed hard on concrete. Some springboard.

We didn't call it quits quite yet, though. Our schedule included more meetings. I would keep trying to try.

That August, after I received the official ALS diagnosis from Dr. Rothstein at Johns Hopkins and shared the news with my family in St. Louis, Eve and I went to Wisconsin. It was just before my 34th birthday. I struggled to get down the hill from the house to the lake. I couldn't fish anymore. I was scared to go swimming lest I slip on the sandy-muddy lake bottom and not have enough arm strength to keep my head above the water. I couldn't shoo away the mosquitoes and horseflies. The woods became menacing. The flies would bite. I wanted to swat them, relieve the sting on my sweaty skin, but my arms, nearly useless, couldn't threaten them. Insects buzzed at my ear, seemed to find my skin sweet. Later, in the refuge of her parents' screen porch, Eve would swab tea tree oil on my swollen spots.

On Sunday morning, Eve and her parents left for church. I planned to spend a few hours staring at the lake and watching the fish look for breakfast. I grabbed a newspaper to read and turned to the business section where I found an article about how the economy was heading into a recession. I knew that one of the first types of investment to drop off in a recession is "risk capital" – precisely the kind of funding we were trying to raise for iSpringboard. A few months earlier, one of the companies we were advising had gone bankrupt. The opportunity Connie and I had been chasing was evaporating. I couldn't fish and I couldn't shoo away flies; I couldn't write and I couldn't lift my own weight; but I could read the newspaper, and knew then what I had to do.

I walked up from the lake to the screen porch of the house, sat in one of the wicker chairs, and dialed the telephone. Connie answered. We chatted briefly and then I made my pitch.

"You know, with a recession coming, things could get pretty ugly," I said.

"What do you mean?"

"If there's a recession, we might lose even more of the companies we've been advising. And if they go, it's going to be an uphill climb to launch this fund. And..."

"And if there's no fund there won't be any money to pay either of us."

"And you could find yourself stuck in a big mortgage, having to choose between burning through your savings or a firesale of your dreamhouse."

Connie doesn't share her disappointment with others. She had probably come to a similar conclusion already, because on the call she agreed rather matter-of-factly that it was time to end iSpringboard. Even if we'd had investors clamoring to sign on immediately, my condition raised an ethical issue. I didn't feel right convincing someone to invest in me when I didn't have a reasonable expectation I would be able to manage that investment.

After hanging up, I walked gingerly back down to the lake, sat on a bench near the water, and tried not to panic. For the first time in my life I didn't have a plan. I tried not to think about becoming useless, with no viable tasks or work, no way to earn a living. I tried not to think about becoming dependent and unable to care for myself. Did I still have a future, even if it was terribly shorter than I had ever imagined? I pictured a springboard, a figure launched upward, buoyant and airborne. Where would I fly if not along the life trajectory I had planned? How could I stop in mid-air and change direction? The future I wanted had slipped away, and with it, every dream I had about what might have been.

After that vacation in Wisconsin, Eve and I returned to San Francisco. I still felt adrift, trying to quell my panic, but I had begun thinking. The misery that accompanied my descent toward a definitive diagnosis was something I could soften, or at least address, through a goal. iSpringboard had been one such goal; challenging, complex, and potentially lucrative. Building it gave me an escape from the darkness of having a terminal illness. But meaninglessness is a much tougher problem. With a few exceptions, like the well-paying jobs I had helped create in Moscow, I had spent most of my life working to improve my own prosperity. I didn't think this was intrinsically wrong, from a moral perspective, because I planned to address it later in life. My long-term plan had been to make enough money not to have to think about it anymore, and then apply the experience I had gained from building new companies, especially raising money for them, in some charitable context. When I thought I had another fifty years to fulfill that plan, I saw nothing wrong with my choices. But what if it was more like three to five?

One cool August morning back in San Francisco I took Ike for a walk, and when we returned I went to the bathroom to get cleaned up. I couldn't lift my arms high enough to pull off my t-shirt, so I positioned them on the counter by the sink, and carefully knelt so my elbows would stay on the counter. Then I ducked my head and let my forearms flop onto the neck of the t-shirt. I grabbed as much material as I could and stood up. As my arms fell forward I wiggled a little and the shirt came off. From one of the cabinet drawers I grabbed my electric razor. The mirror over the sink was too far away to see my stubble so I turned around to face a full-length mirror built into the opposite wall. By then I couldn't hold my hands up to my face for more than a few seconds before my biceps would start to shake.

I held the razor in both hands like a normal person might hold a heavy bag of flour, and leaned my arms against the mirror to keep them steady. Then I flicked on the power and moved my face around the razor to shave. When I finished I stepped back to put the razor in a drawer but stopped when I caught a view of my shoulders in the mirror. Of course I understood that my shoulders were atrophying, but every day I told myself they looked the same as they had the day before. That morning I stared. My shoulders were bony. I had been consumed with fears about my changing musculature for months, bargaining with my arms, saying to them, "If you would just stop changing I could happily live for the rest of my life with you as you are now."

I had been clinging to an image of myself that was fast slipping away. As I stared at myself in the mirror I wondered what would happen if I dropped dead on the floor right then and there. What would my life have been? I would have spent thirty-four years entirely devoted to myself, devoid of any real meaning or significance, and the last many months in total misery. Whether I died that moment or slid slowly toward my end, I finally understood that only I could change how much meaning there would be in my life. And if I truly did not have decades to fix it, I was making it miserable, wasting very precious time feeling sorry for myself and not doing anything.

I stared at my face in the mirror and thought, "Get busy you fool."

Chapter Seven

Extra Hands for ALS

◆◆◆◆◆◆◆

"I have some bad news to share with you," I began. After hiding from my friends for more than a year, at last I was ready to tell them why. Since that crucial moment staring at myself in the mirror, when I realized that I am the only one who could give my life meaning, I had indeed gotten busy, and gone to work. I began by sending an e-mail to my friends announcing my illness. I apologized for being out of touch for so long, and then keeping things brief and factual, I explained my symptoms and ALS diagnosis. Although my news shocked and saddened them, almost everyone responded by asking what they could do to help. I spent most of the next month catching up with friends, many of whom flew out to San Francisco just to give me a hug. I had switched to Dr. Olney's care by then, and he had prescribed various drugs, some that might slow the progression of the disease, and others to help control my symptoms.

Although most of my symptoms were not immediately noticeable, they did surface occasionally. One weekend, Eve's college roommate and her boyfriend came to visit. We were on our way to the San Francisco Zoo when Eve's roommate described her recent experiences working as an ob/gyn resident. She was complaining about the long, sleepless, 36-hour stints on call at the hospital, telling us how unnecessary they seemed to her training.

"Obstetrics?" I asked, intentionally making myself sound puzzled. "I thought you said you were on call three times a week."

She looked at me, her eyebrows twisted. "Yeah, I am on call three times a week."

"Doesn't that mean you're an on-call-ogist?"

She smiled broadly at my joke and chuckled. Her boyfriend and Eve also snickered. Meanwhile, I laughed, hard. No, I guffawed. I laughed so hard my abs burned and my eyes watered.

The three of them looked at me. The joke was cute, but it certainly didn't merit my reaction. In my mind I thought, "Jack, chill out. It's not that funny." Eve tugged at my shirtsleeve and her look said, "OK, Jack, enough." Laughter poured out of me like the foam from a bottle of champagne; it kept coming after the initial burst, dribbling, making me terribly embarrassed and self-conscious.

I had felt the same thing before, ever since the onset of my symptoms, and it had frightened me. At first, I found myself laughing too much, then getting choked up after seeing a Coke commercial. I wondered, "What the hell is wrong with me?! Am I losing my mind?" It seemed strange that I could lose my mind but be aware of it at the same time. Surely, the fact that I could even pose the question indicated the answer was no, right?

Before long I couldn't get a punchline out at all. My mouth would pull into an uncontrollable smile despite chomping down on my lips to try to stop it. And then it spread beyond jokes and commercials. If Eve and I fought about anything, major or minor, I would smile involuntarily which just increased the tension between us, as if I could not take her seriously. I tried to avert my eyes during a tense conversation, picturing in my mind the moment Ike got hit by the police car, but nothing helped enough to enable normal conversation.

In the months I had spent scouring the web reading about ALS I found an explanation for my laughing fits. It's called emotional lability, a symptom typical of various illnesses in which neurons in the brain are damaged such as ALS, Alzheimer's, and stroke. Regardless of the science, I couldn't help but draw metaphoric conclusions. I had bottled up my emotions for as long as I could, and now, uncorked, they were pouring out in a relentless stream. And as much as it was haunting to lose control over my emotional responses while remaining entirely aware of what was happening, I also felt the celebratory air of a champagne party, my spewing emotions a celebration of my emergence from self-imposed exile and secrecy. It meant I was no longer alone with my illness.

Even so, with more friends coming out to visit, I didn't want to act like a cackling jester so I eagerly enrolled in one of Dr. Olney's drug trials involving a combination of dextromethorphan, an ingredient in cough medicine, and quinidine, a compound related to quinine, an ingredient in tonic water. He said I might experience increased muscle stiffness as a side effect, but that seemed a small price to pay for "comic relief."

Within a few days of taking the new pills I felt different. At moments when I used to burst out laughing I could feel that urge coming on but subsiding. I felt a little stiffer than usual, particularly in my jaw, but that seemed an even trade to be returned to near-normalcy. A week or so later, Eve and I took some friends visiting from New York out to dinner. We drove to the restaurant but had to park several blocks away. My legs were still strong so I didn't worry about having to walk. As we crossed the street a stiff, foggy-wet breeze whipped into me. It froze me solid, as if it had been composed of liquid nitrogen. Every muscle in my body flexed involuntarily at the same time and I couldn't relax them. If Eve had not been holding my arm, my momentum would have carried me forward and I would have toppled like a statue.

"What's wrong?" Eve asked.

I tried to say, "I don't know," but with my jaw locked shut I managed to say only, "N dnn't nnnn." With help from our guests, I tottered to the sidewalk. When it became obvious I couldn't walk the next four blocks, not to mention the next four feet, Eve pulled the car over and stuffed me in front of the heaters. As she drove to the restaurant, I thawed.

I was volatile alright, one week laughing uncontrollably and the next week frozen to an ice block. But the outpouring of affection I received from my friends in visits, phone calls, and e-mails was one of the most moving experiences of my life. It made me think that if I could find a way to spark a similar reaction from the friends of people with ALS everywhere, I might be able to make a major contribution to the fight against ALS.

I began to dream, then, about using my skills to raise money to fund research that could help ALS patients. I spoke with Connie, to whom I explained what I saw as the underlying issues – because ALS is relatively rare, discoveries in the basic science of the disease do not automatically translate into effective therapies because drug makers cannot rationally divert their research budgets away from therapies for health issues that affect more people. The common sense of this is irrefutable. If you had to decide how to allocate a finite research budget across seasonal allergies, the common cold, heartburn, and ALS, your shareholders would demand that you focus on the first three. Health issues affecting small numbers of people simply do not attract the interest of the pharmaceutical industry. As a result they are referred to as orphan diseases. As I saw it, this is a market failure with almost no remedy.

After listening to me talk, Connie, as insightful as always, said, "If the only way to attract therapeutic research dollars to ALS is to increase the numbers of people living with the disease, then you'll have to find a way to keep them alive longer. That will be expensive, so where will you find that much money?"

Connie was right. I kept thinking, and talking, and dreaming. Then I heard about Jamie Heywood and his organization, the ALS Therapy Development Institute. His model seemed exactly on point. Jamie's brother, Stephen Heywood, had been diagnosed at the age of twenty-nine. Jamie responded with heroic feats of heart and mind in the hope of finding a way to extend his brother's life. When I first heard about the organization he had created, Jamie's team was conducting tests on ALS mice using drugs the Food and Drug Administration had approved for any health issue that shared the pathogenesis of ALS. If any one of the drugs being tested on mice could slow or arrest the progression of ALS, the fact that there was already abundant data on human safety meant they could be prescribed immediately for people with ALS. Instead of spending hundreds of millions of dollars to create a new compound and usher it through years of animal and human tests, the process at the ALS Therapy Development Institute could potentially reveal a drug for less than $50,000, and after only months of testing. Jamie's model was revolutionary.

I scheduled a visit to Boston to meet Jamie. Six weeks earlier I had felt weighed down under a wet blanket of despair, but now, every day, I felt a little lighter. I spent all day e-mailing, reading, calling, thinking, and planning. I had a new purpose, one that could occupy and channel my emotions in the way iSpringboard had done, but this time I was not only busy but my activities felt meaningful.

Eve and I flew to Boston in mid-October when New England is lit up, the foliage fiery red and burnt orange. I had expected Jamie Heywood to be an older guy, a grey-haired scientist, but in fact he is much more like me. We are the same age, and both have a boyish face on a tall, lanky body. We both use humor, sometimes of the blackest sort, to deal with the seriousness of terminal illness. And we are both completely devoted to our work. The day we met we connected immediately. He toured Eve and me around his offices introducing us to his staff. They were almost all young, intelligent, and inspired, their offices small and tight, much like mine had been in Russia. I felt at home.

Half an hour into meeting with Jamie, I was startled to see someone familiar walk through the door. "Chris?" I said. "What are you doing here?" It was Chris Hobler, from St. Louis, who had been two years ahead of me in high school.

Chris didn't say anything. He pointed to his mouth and shook his head, then held up his index finger and tapped, slowly, on his thumb, the secret handshake of our unfortunate club. His brother, Peter, explained that Chris had lost his voice to ALS over the previous nine months; in fact his voice had been the first thing to go. His disease is referred to as bulbar-onset ALS, because the first symptoms appear in the areas controlled by the bulbar region of the brain—the lower face and neck. People with bulbar-onset ALS lose the ability to speak, chew, and swallow rather quickly, and tend to have a faster overall progression. Chris walked over and greeted me with a hug. He and his brother had heard about me through the St. Louis grapevine a week or two earlier. Judging from the strength of his hug which enveloped me, he had not lost much other function besides his voice. In comparison, I felt like a stick figure.

Chris and his brother had also come to meet Jamie and to talk about fundraising for ALS. That first day we spent hours talking about what we could do, individually and collectively, to raise money for research. The second day Jamie took Eve and me on a tour of their laboratory, rented from the Massachusetts College of Pharmacology. Up a flight of stairs, around a few corners, and past a battery of double doors we walked into a wall of odor, the stench of hundreds of mice. The drugs Jamie hoped would help prolong the life of his brother were being screened in this lab. I looked at the mice in their cages, their beady eyes and swishing tails, some of them weak like me, all of them quiet like Chris. As I listened to the competent seriousness with which the lab staff explained their testing and evaluation methods, I felt drawn in to Jamie's vision, and that if science had an answer waiting for me Jamie's team would find it.

I left Boston with a clearer idea of what I wanted to do. Six weeks later, on December 5th, I announced the launch of what I called "my latest startup" in an e-mail I sent to everyone who had been so supportive of me since I had revealed my illness. It was a thrilling moment. There was nothing left of the rudderless drift I had felt by the lake in Wisconsin after having dropped iSpringboard.

My friends responded to the email I sent with contributions totaling more than $25,000, enough to say the Jack Orchard ALS Foundation was open for business. But I still had no answer for Connie's essential question: How could I reach and earn the support of the thousands of people with ALS and their families?

A week later I received an e-mail from Harry's wife, Betsy Orchard. She suggested I contact the high school we had both attended, John Burroughs School, to see if we could get one or two seniors, who are required to spend May volunteering in the community, to work with me. I thought Betsy's idea was interesting, and drafted a proposal to make an arrangement with the school that would be enticing for the students. Over the next few months, I refined the proposal and discussed it with a core group of my friends. I heard the wheels of my new start-up venture beginning to turn, still creaky and slow.

Then one day when I was at Dr. Olney's clinic at the University of California San Francisco Medical Center, all the loose strands of ideas I had been collecting about how to answer Connie's question came together. My fundraising success had earned an invitation to join the Advisory Board of Olney's clinic; that day I happened to read an article posted on a bulletin board in the waiting room. The article described two college students who had worked with clinic staff to organize companionship visits to people homebound with ALS. I looked at the faces of the smiling college students in the picture; one wearing a red sweatshirt, the other in shorts and a striped t-shirt; and I saw their strength and eagerness. Suddenly, I realized I had found the answer to Connie's question.

I could organize student volunteers to help ALS families! They could spend two hours each week helping around the house, shouldering some of the caregiver's burden, and lending their hands to the person with ALS to read Sports Illustrated, or organize a photo album, or a thousand other tasks to give him an escape from thoughts about mortality. Simple and elegant, this structure could give patients additional pur-

pose in their lives by turning them into teachers, show-
ing young people how to face news of the worst sort
with grace and repose. It could give family caregivers
time for a meal with a friend, or a good book, or
maybe just a nap. Meanwhile, it could give the students opportunities to grow and mature through an
emotionally challenging experience, to understand
how powerfully they can impact other people's lives
by doing simple things for them, and to gain self-
confidence as they learn about their own inner
strength. Then, working together with other students
to educate their peers and communities about ALS
through public awareness initiatives, they could develop and apply leadership skills.

Yes, the home visit could benefit everyone involved. Working with and through students, I would
reach people with ALS all over the country and then
inspire their friends to react as mine had. We named
the program Extra Hands for ALS.

And why stop at ALS? Wouldn't Extra Hands
for Parkinson's work just as effectively as a youth development program and a patient service? And Extra
Hands for Alzheimer's? And multiple sclerosis? And
stroke? Why not Extra Hands for every family that
needs help in the home due to a disabling condition?
As the baby boomers age they'll explode the number
of disabled people in our country. Without sufficient
numbers of home health aides ready to care for them,
the cost of home care will soar. The cost to the nation
will also increase dramatically as family caregivers
leave their jobs to take care of disabled loved ones.
But what if Extra Hands could send a couple pairs of

students into every one of those homes? Couldn't it soften the economic effects of the coming crisis while simultaneously teaching our country's young people about the importance of community service? The long-term potential of the Extra Hands concept seemed limitless.

The home visit also answered the vexing issue of finding meaning in my own life. I had never looked for it through spirituality. Even when the neurologist handed down my death sentence I felt no urge to withdraw into faith. But still I needed to know that my life, however short it might be, had meaning. Reading that article I felt my life come full circle from my Sunday mornings with Rabbi Rosenbloom so many years earlier. In his sermons, among the clods of spirituality I often found shards of an ancient vessel, bits and pieces scattered about that, at the time, I could not assemble with so little life experience. I knew what I believed but not how to apply my beliefs in a way that would imbue my life with feelings of richness, significance, and righteousness. But twenty years later, there in that article lay the answer how to fit them together.

The shards the rabbi described were principles underlying human civilization – commitment to community, appreciation for behavior consistent with peaceful coexistence, respect for diversity, desire to promote growth and prosperity for both the individual and the community, and conviction that ethical conduct can be judged by its ability to enhance the individual's and the community's well-being at the same time. If these shards were assembled one way, the resulting vessel looked very much like the morality embedded in Judeo-Christian theology, glued together with the mysticism of spiritual faith. But they could also fit together another way, held in place by the fact that humans are social animals, needing and yet competing with each other to assure our progeny a prosperous future.

Once assembled, this vessel held the answer I needed to find. By bringing out the best in students, I could make it possible for people with ALS to enjoy fruitful, meaningful lives despite their condition or the little time they have left. Their example would influence the students for the rest of their lives, giving them an appreciation for their ability to improve their communities – and in so doing – their own lives.

And what if everyone practiced this, working to bring out the best in others? Then everyone would achieve the best in life. But do we have to live in a utopian society, where we all give up our jobs and go to work for charities, to realize such a vision? I don't think so. Among other things, we don't all agree on how to bring out the best in other people. You might believe the best way to do it would be through your church or synagogue, wrapped up in spirituality, while others might have a different idea.

For me, the simplicity of the Extra Hands model held vast potential to reach across religions and dissolve dividing lines between people of different belief systems. In fact, that is what I found most compelling about it. I realized then that if I could use my gifts, those ALS would not strip from me, to build something that would enact this simple philosophy and draw in people of all beliefs, I would be able to die with the knowledge that my time had been purposeful and impactful.

"Good morning. I'm Jack Orchard. I'm 35 years old and I'm going to die before most of you graduate." In September 2002, a year after my shaving epiphany, I sat on the stage of John Burroughs School, the high school I attended in St. Louis, speaking to the assembled student body and faculty. I had not visited the school in many years but not much had changed besides the students' attire. The dress code prohibits bare feet in the buildings, but judging from the bare midriffs I saw on the gangly, gawky girls, that was about it. I had dressed casually for my presentation, a turtleneck and some old chinos, because I didn't want to draw dividing lines between the students and myself. In fact, I wanted exactly the opposite. I wanted to show them ALS could strike anyone.

Strange as it may seem, during the eighteen years since I graduated from Burroughs, I had often visualized myself presenting from this lectern before giving a speech or pitching a new investment. Great athletes say the secret behind honing their technique is to visualize it in advance, to "feel" every muscle group in motion in their minds first, and then bring it to life on the playing field. Ironic as it may be for someone whose actual muscles are progressively weakening, I thought of this visualization technique as I prepared to address the students. With its polished wood floors and heavy blue velvet drapes the stage was familiar, even if it looked smaller than I remembered. I had been in the school musical a few times, and I had played there with my band, the Bedspins, in which I sang lead vocals. We had rocked the house with covers of the Rolling Stones and the Who. As an adult, I had made hundreds of presentations, many to tough audiences and from bigger stages than this high school, but still, I was nervous. I wanted more than just for the students to hear me. I wanted them to feel a deep connection to me, to identify with me.

The gentle murmur that pervaded the auditorium as the students filed in had turned to utter silence when I introduced myself. Now that I had their attention I moved on, tearing down any perceived barriers between them and me. "Eighteen years ago I sat out there where you are, sometimes listening, sometimes just finishing my homework." They chuckled a little. Then Eve clicked to the first slide of our presentation, a picture of me and three friends, all in the Burroughs blue, gold, and white football uniforms, smiling proudly, and holding our fingers up to say we're number one. "That's me on the right, the one with the red hair and the goofy smile," I said, trying to keep my voice steady. "That was taken in November 1984, moments after we had whipped Country Day."

Just a few weeks before their homecoming, they liked hearing about defeating their archrival school, even if it happened before their time. "I'm here today to ask you to join me in building something special and unprecedented, something which will make a difference." I talked about ALS and explained the Extra Hands program. "We plan to open chapters all across the country," I said. "You can be part of a national movement to fight this horrible disease." I ended my presentation by announcing that Eve and I would be in the auditorium foyer afterwards to answer questions, and we would leave application forms with the faculty coordinator so those who wanted to think about our invitation could take the time they needed.

We never got a chance to leave the stage. Dozens of students raced down the aisles to meet us. I was astonished. Feeling optimistic, we had brought fifty application forms, but there were so many outstretched hands the forms disappeared in minutes. I thought, "We're going to need a bigger training room." I didn't have long to think, however, because so many students wanted to introduce themselves and, eyes opened wide, they said they wanted to help. I had forgotten how idealistic and impassioned teenagers can be when they're not posturing, and how genuine they can be when you ask something serious of them.

Later, as we pulled out of the parking lot, I was flooded by a sense of accomplishment and gratitude. I had worked so hard and climbed so far from despair to reach this moment, but that wasn't what made it so fulfilling. Was it the feeling that I had reached the next generation, one that would continue when I am gone? Was it the sense that I had found a way to transform my personal catastrophe into a tool for helping others? I felt in touch with my best self that morning, and I felt more successful than I ever had in my life before my ALS diagnosis. Besides, we had rocked the house.

I had been right about one thing. We would need a bigger training room to accommodate the dozens of John Burroughs School volunteers who had raced down the aisles to meet Eve and me. We also had to address the fact that we had many more volunteers than we could match with ALS families, and we didn't want to waste the enthusiasm we had whipped up at the school. So we decided to train them all and offer more than one pair of helpers to the half-dozen families who had registered in the program.

I was looking forward to the training session, in part to share in the students' enthusiasm and in part to correct a mistake we had made at the first one, which had taken place three months earlier, in July 2002, to run a pilot program to test our concept. That training session took place in a spacious but dark conference room offered by the ALS Association, a national organization whose St. Louis chapter had agreed to help us get started. I remember sitting at the meeting table looking at the walls which were covered with the names of people who had died of ALS, hundreds of names of people whose only remaining public memory was buried in a list taped to a wall in a quiet office building. It was a somber atmosphere. And then in came an ALS patient, an older woman whose grown daughter had to help her maneuver her wheelchair. This woman rolled up directly across from me and immediately glanced at my withered hands.

"You have it too?" she asked. She seemed surprised, not just that someone decades younger than she could share her predicament, but that anyone could. I knew from her daughter that she hadn't left home since her diagnosis six months earlier. Perhaps her self-imposed isolation had skewed her thinking? I certainly knew what that was like from my own dark time. But everyone else in the room, including the six timid, fresh-faced girls, our very first volunteers, had been sitting quietly, so the woman's question pierced the hushed room like the first serve at Wimbledon. All heads turned to see how I would return the serve. Because I didn't want to disrupt the training agenda, I just stuck out my racquet.

"Yes," I said. All heads turned back to the woman.

"Where do you have it, just the hands?" she asked. Her question skipped across the court, a challenging shot. In fact, I had some impairment in almost every part of my body by then. But I did not want to dive for my return, so again I just said, "Yes." Now she raced to the net.

"I got it in the legs but I'm starting to feel it in my hands now, too." That was too much for me. The meeting was not intended to be a support group, just an orientation. We had thought it would help the volunteers to meet people with ALS to reduce their first-visit jitters. But if anything, the macabre volley only heightened their anxiety. I turned to Eve and said, "Let's get started."

At the time, I moved on past that uncomfortable exchange as fast as I could, but it held a deeper lesson I could only grasp in retrospect. The woman's neediness had been palpable, from her wheelchair to her tone of voice, but probably not greatly different than my own. The biggest difference between us was that I worked assiduously to hide my neediness. By that point, I could not lift or carry anything, but I always clasped my hands together in my lap to avoid having them hang limply off the ends of chair arms. My legs had been so strong from years of Stairmastering that, even weakened, I could still stand and walk independently, but when I used a wheelchair I would transfer to a regular chair when I reached my destination and tuck the wheelchair away out of sight. So as I sat there in the meeting room, doing everything I could to avoid drifting into difficult emotional territory, in fact I was allowing a powerful irony to persist – that as much as I was thriving as the founder of Extra Hands for ALS, and was acutely aware of how ALS sufferers need extra hands, I was blind to my own needs, or more accurately, to Eve's needs as she tried to manage mine.

Just as I had incrementally lost my physical abilities, she had incrementally gained responsibility. The fact of Eve's ever-increasing burden lay right in front of me, like sitting so close to a television that all you can see are red, green, and blue pixels dancing about. I might have been setting up this new organization, but Eve was setting me up each day and working to build Extra Hands right in front of me. Before long she ran out of time to pay attention to everything else important to her. But at the time I just saw red, green, and blue.

Chapter Eight

Believe!

◆◆◆◆◆◆◆

'MIRACLE MOM SAVES CHILD.' Before my diagnosis, when I was still living in San Francisco, this small item in the newspaper caught my eye. Perhaps because in those days I was brooding about my disappearing muscle strength, I found myself reading about a toddler who ran into the street and was somehow caught beneath a Ford Escort. The driver had managed to stop short before he crushed the child, and the mother, who had momentarily turned to stir something on the stove, only to see the car roll over her child, dashed out of the house and into the street, where she lifted the car the few inches off the ground required to save her child. Although the driver and the gawking neighbors were hysterical with fear and grief, a tremendous calm seemed to accompany the mother's strength.

Scientists explain this strength as a rush of adrenaline. Danger provoked the mother's adrenal gland to flood her body, which in turn increased her heart rate, dilated her pupils, and gave her, momentarily at least, tremendous strength. She felt no pain. She knew no reason. She saw her daughter in need of saving and saved her.

Spiritual people attribute this strength to God, a miracle, a sign, an angel's intervention. And yet since the onset of my illness, I have wondered – and people have often asked – where do I find strength? How do I keep going?

In April 2002, I sat in my study in San Francisco as light streamed through the window and dust motes danced. With half-full brown cardboard boxes at my feet, I looked across the half-empty bookshelves wondering which volume should go in the boxes next. By then, my symptoms had turned our three-story dream house into an obstacle course, both physically and financially; and we knew this would only worsen with time. The time to leave had obviously come.

Moving to St. Louis had been Eve's idea. In St. Louis, she and I could be near my family, and we could live much more cheaply. She wanted to be able to rely on the assistance of my family. But after decades of obstinately asserting my independence, venturing out in the world, and guarding my privacy tightly, I simply could not see myself asking, for example, my younger brother, Harry, to take me to the bathroom or clean out my stuffy nose. It didn't matter that he did the same for his children every day, but that he had looked up to me all through our childhood years.

I remember one evening at summer camp in Wisconsin when he was homesick. He was ten years old, and it was his first trip away from home for more than a night. He walked into my cabin with tears welling in his eyes, told me how his cabin counselor had hurt his feelings, and that he wanted to go home. I understood because the same thing had happened to me two years earlier. We talked about his jerky counselor, and how we might seek revenge by short-sheeting his bed. Harry laughed at the thought of a little mischief; he still does actually. Soon he felt better and went on his way.

As children I had been Harry's "big brother," the one he revered, and he had been my "little brother," the one I didn't want wearing the same clothes as me, or going wherever I went, or touching my stuff. Although Harry and I have always been very close, these roles, indeed all our intra-family relationships, became part of our identities. To change them meant relinquishing those parts of my identity. Having already lost so much of my self-image, now it was painful to permit my family members' relationships with me to change.

Sitting in my study, I looked at my well-worn philosophy books. As a college student I had taken a few courses in the philosophy department, and although I enjoyed them, I failed to understand how some ideas scratched onto parchment centuries ago related to me or the life I wanted to live. As a healthy 21-year old college senior I didn't have much reason to look for such connections. My days were filled with studying for exams, preparing for job interviews, and gobbling Chinese take-out – the mundane minutia of the daily life of someone with a long future ahead of him. But as I grew weaker, the connections between those deep thoughts and my need to find meaning in my life became clearer and much more important with every day spent at my desk nurturing Extra Hands.

Regardless of your spirituality, an encounter with your mortality will force you to ask yourself what you believe, and to ponder how far away that is from what you know for a fact. Because my worldview centers on that which is empirically provable, I felt drawn to the works of philosophers who had grappled with the distinction between faith and science.

One of the philosophers whose works I studied was a public servant and lawyer in 16th century France. Michel de Montaigne lived during a time of great upheaval, particularly with respect to the Church, but also in the way western civilization understood itself. The splintering of the Church into numerous religions, each offering the sole path to salvation, stirred doubts that any of them may truly know the way to eternal bliss. Simultaneously, the discovery of thriving cultures in the "New World," societies built entirely outside Christiandom, led de Montaigne and others to question the primacy of western culture. When in 1580 he wrote in one of his Essays, "What do I know?" he was in fact asking how to distinguish absolute truth from accepted belief and habit. Eventually he settled on a maxim: no culture has the right to impose its beliefs and values on others if those beliefs and values are based on cultural habit rather than truth or fact. In our modern world, stuffed full as it is with the fruits of scientific experimentation and discovery, it's easy to forget that we owe a part of our way of life to Michel de Montaigne, the first person after the Dark Ages to acknowledge the importance of the freedom of inquiry.

In my condition now, still and silent, I ask myself what I believe every day. And each day I feel more certain that I have found no new revelations. Instead, I have grown ever more convinced that, working together, we are capable of magnificent acts of courage and fortitude to improve our individual and collective lives. It's called humanism, the belief that we need only to look to ourselves in the search for answers to questions big and small, empirical and theoretical, existential and ontological.

Yes, humanism – with its commitment to the use of reason and scientific method in fashioning solutions to human problems, its steady quest for objective truth, its pursuit of principles of ethical conduct without a divine inspiration, and its concern for the fulfillment and enrichment of the lives of individuals and their communities – is the source of my strength, the foundation of my faith.

Looking at my philosophy books, I thought about what I had learned from them – a deeply held conviction that even if I could not pack them with my clumsy hands, I could still find the strength to build Extra Hands for ALS because it enacts the central feature of humanism, our human responsibility to each other, to making community here on earth in this life.

In St. Louis in June 2002, Eve and I rented a house on a quiet street in the suburbs just a few miles from the house where I grew up. It was a ranch house with three bedrooms on a quarter of an acre with a fenced-in back yard, perfect for Ike to roam around, chase squirrels, and flirt with the neighbor's poodle.

We were situated in a part of the city called Creve Coeur, so if you speak a little French and mispronounce the name of the state, you could say we lived in Broken Heart, Misery.

That spring and summer, though, Eve and I felt optimistic rather than broken hearted. We loved the sun room in the back of the house with its big windows, French doors, and fireplace. It had a deck outside the west doors, with a beautiful redbud tree hanging over it, and a spacious patio outside the east doors. We set up our office in there, with Eve and me on opposite sides of our desk. We used the small dining room as a meeting room, with a conference phone as a centerpiece, and the open living room/kitchen as Ike's romper room. Eve planted an organic vegetable garden in back that produced tomatoes enough for the entire neighborhood, as well as cucumbers, bell peppers, soybeans, peas, carrots, squash, eggplant, and watermelon. I loved going out there to see the bounty her hard work had produced.

That first year in St. Louis, our life proved bountiful, too. Eve and I usually finished getting me ready around nine o'clock. Then I would wander into the sun room and plop down in my office chair, ready to begin a day of emailing, phone calling, and nurturing Extra Hands and the Jack Orchard ALS Foundation. I could almost believe we were back in Moscow, where Eve and I had first worked together and where I had last known the heady rush that accompanies a new venture.

We were definitely not in Moscow, though, where I worked out at the gym and could walk for miles; we were in Missouri, where some months after the move, my arms became too weak for me to be independent anymore. Working together masked how dependent on Eve I had become. If I had scheduled a meeting outside the house she would go with me, helping me in and out of a jacket, the car, a chair, and then in reverse on the way home.

One evening I wanted to go to an ALS fundraiser organized by my friend Chris Hobler, but the event was scheduled at the same time as Eve's favorite yoga class.

"It's important for us to be there," I said. "Chris and his family are expecting us."

"But this is Tuesday night," she replied. "It's the same class I go to every Tuesday."

"Eve, we've known about this fundraiser for weeks. Can't you go to a class that meets in the afternoon?" I felt angry and disappointed, and my face showed it.

"No," she said. "The best teacher leads the one tonight. It's just two nights a week, and we've talked about getting your family to help you occasionally or hiring someone to…"

"My family is busy enough, and you know how I feel about hiring strangers to come over here," I said. She could not be convinced. I would have to get someone else to take me. As she drove away to her class, I scooted my chair over to the speakerphone and dialed a friend's number. By then my arms had become nearly useless. To make a phone call I had to lean over the phone and tap the numbers with my nose.

Buoyed by Michel de Montaigne and the pantheon of philosophers whose ideas formed the underpinning of humanism, I found strength to keep going, day after day, despite my quadriplegia. My humanist convictions, especially my realization that only I could make my life meaningful, enabled me to set aside thoughts of my impending demise and focus on nurturing Extra Hands for ALS from an idea to a successful national charity. Its ability to benefit everyone involved in it became addictive for me, something I couldn't set aside because the more time I spent working on it, the more fulfilled I felt.

I hope that in the way Extra Hands enriches my life, it will do the same for you, and for anyone searching for meaning no matter what their spiritual views may be. I have put so much work into building it precisely because my end is near, and I want to know that I have left behind something of value, something you and others can use to find some measure of the peace I have found.

Although I am proud of various achievements from my first thirty-four years, in general they are neither original nor distinguishing. Extra Hands, however, is both, and it produces new results every day that make me even prouder. Some of the most important, to me, are the simplest. At one of the first Extra Hands student training sessions, a 16-year old girl named Sarah was so shy she could not even look Eve in the eye to say hello. Her voice was barely audible. We wondered if we should accept her into the program at all for fear that someone so seemingly fragile might not cope well in the home of a terminally ill person.

But we paired her with another student with a more extroverted personality, and assigned her a Mentor, an adult volunteer whose function is to supervise and counsel the students, who had lost a parent to ALS. Then we assigned this team to help a single mother with ALS whose 9-year old daughter greatly needed a degree of normalcy in her life. Three months later, as we prepared to film recruiting videos, we were shocked to discover that Sarah wanted to be interviewed on camera. I'll never forget what she said when the interviewer asked her what she had learned through her Extra Hands experience: "[The person I visit] is so filled with courage and determination, and to see how determined she is has really made me realize how determined I can be with everything I do." I nearly fell out of my seat with excitement. I wanted to shout, "YES! YOU GOT IT!"

The students are not the only beneficiaries of Extra Hands. It has had a powerful impact on many of the ALS families who have joined, perhaps none moreso than a person who emailed me in 2005. I usually pass emails asking about the Extra Hands program to one of the people on my team, but I always answer questions myself from people with ALS or their families. In 2005, a man with ALS who had run out of money expressed how emotionally difficult it was to keep living while knowing his children were paying his way even though they could not afford it. I replied with a few ideas about what he could do to ease his financial situation, and then received this e-mail from him a few months later:

"Hi Jack, this is a note to tell you that you've helped me to avoid suicide. I'm not going to do it now. I had a plan but your inspiration led me to believe that I have hope."

Like the person who sent me this very touching note, I have struggled mightily with accepting help from others without seeing it as diminishing my dignity. I suppose everyone defines dignity in their own way, but I would bet my definition is commonly held: I deserve to be respected in mind and body. My thoughts and opinions are worthy of consideration automatically, and regardless of my changing ability to express them, my body is not an object to be handled or acted upon without that consideration.

I don't know where our culture fashioned its typical definition of dignity, but I do know that when I finally hired my first personal aide I held on to it with all the strength I could muster. I still felt embarrassed having anyone but Eve help me in the bathroom. And it irked me that the home health agency mandated we hire an aide in four-hour increments, which meant I paid a lot of money for someone to feed me a sandwich for ten minutes and then sit around for the remainder of the shift.

In June 2003 I hired my first full-time personal aide. While most of the applicants for the position we advertised in the newspaper came dressed in hospital scrubs and lacking credentials, Jennifer appeared dressed for an interview with a resume and typed list of references. She is tall and strong, so walking with her steadying me was an entirely different experience than leaning on Eve, nine inches shorter and much lighter than I. I noticed her hands, always manicured, strong hands that pulled me out of bed, and set me in my chair. Nimble hands that buttoned and zipped, smoothed and shaved, fried up a couple eggs and lifted a fork to my mouth. Hands that fluttered as she strapped me into a seatbelt and hands that slammed shut the car door and then took the wheel in their strong grip. At first they seemed animated, her hands, not in the way of a Hindu goddess, but hands that were alive because I could now receive what they had to give.

The first morning Jennifer came to get me up, it was a gorgeous summer day. She arrived at eight o'clock, whisked me out of bed, got me shaved, showered, dressed, and fed, and then drove me to my office where she worked as an assistant for my staff. I felt so enormously relieved to be independent of Eve that I finally understood how foolish I had been not to have taken this step months earlier.

That evening, sitting at my computer writing emails while baseball announcers chattered in the background, I silently ached on the inside. My new aide had given me a level of productivity I had not experienced in more than a year, and although I felt like celebrating the arrival of a new era, I was alone. Eve was out on the town with friends or at yoga class. She left the house most evenings around the time I arrived home from the Extra Hands office. Our life together had shattered, and the love inside it that we once felt for each other had spilled away.

I realized then that my goal had to be to take the help I received – now, from my new caregiver, and also the help from the past, in fact a whole lifetime of help, beginning with my parents, my sister and brothers, then my teachers, professors, lifelong friends, and the new friends who were helping me with Extra Hands – and give that help back, to others. Help, too, from philosophers long since turned to dust but whose words have become eternal, who helped me understand that my life would accrue increasing meaning to the degree I could bring out the best in others. For me, this is a core principle – that we are linked by responsibility to one another as much as we are linked by any genetic code.

Chapter Nine

American Hero

◆◆◆◆◆◆◆

"...of courage undaunted, possessing a firmness and perseverance of purpose which nothing but impossibilities could divert from its direction; ...of sound understanding, and a fidelity to truth..." Thomas Jefferson wrote that about Meriwether Lewis, leader of the Corps of Discovery that set out from St. Louis in 1804 to find a northwest passage to the Pacific. Young and adventurous, tough and determined, smart and resourceful, Captain Lewis was an impressive leader but a troubled man. After his return in 1806 he struggled with manic depression, something he was able to suppress during the expedition probably because he was pre-occupied with achieving his mission. Three years later, at age thirty-five, he committed suicide while en route to Washington to publish his extensive journals from the expedition.

That was the public Lewis. What most people don't know is that, in addition to discovering and documenting over 300 new animal and plant species, he also treated everyone on the expedition with respect and dignity including, quite remarkably, William Clark's slave, York. When Lewis sought a group decision about where to locate their winter camp on the Pacific Ocean, York had a vote equal to the other members of the corps. And when Lewis named streams, mountains, and newly discovered animals and plants after members of the corps, he included York. This kind of inclusiveness would not be mimicked until the Civil Rights Act 160 years later. Meriwether Lewis is a true American hero, a man utterly selfless and courageous; someone who pioneered new territory, geographically and intellectually; who took tremendous risks, physical and emotional, on behalf of his corps and our young country; and who did not quit in the face of an enormous challenge.

I do not consider myself a hero. Yet, for my efforts Volvo of North America honored me with a Volvo For Life Award in 2005, an annual prize given to "everyday heroes – ordinary people who go above and beyond the call of duty to help others." One of the Extra Hands staff had nominated me, and her eloquent profile of me vaulted my candidacy into the top nine finalists out of 4,272 nominations. Extra Hands was guaranteed to receive a $25,000 contribution and major media attention through a celebrity-laden award ceremony in New York. Although I was excited to attend, and even more excited to see Extra Hands in the spotlight, I was also embarrassed by the award. Creating Extra Hands was neither a selfless act, nor a courageous one. On the contrary, I needed it as much, if not more than, any other person the organization has helped. In exactly the same way a spiritual person turns to his faith in a personal crisis, I turned to my own beliefs in mine. For me, it was a question of survival; I needed Extra Hands for ALS as I needed water to live.

I would make the journey to New York as a quadriplegic. The 2,200 mile road trip may not have rivaled Lewis and Clark's 8,000 mile, two-year adventure, but it was certainly an expedition. The trouble with traveling is not so much the journey itself, but what to do once I arrive at the destination. At home I can get comfortable easily and spend hours working at my computer without assistance. But anywhere else, without my equipment, I struggle like the princess and the pea. I can't do anything without help. At home I can also eat properly, which is quite a chore with a tongue that doesn't work well and weak throat muscles. People with such problems often get what is called meal fatigue; you just can't take another bite of whatever you're eating even though you're still hungry. So to get enough calories to maintain your weight, you might have to try several different dishes in one meal. At the time of the road trip to New York, I had just had a feeding tube inserted in my abdomen, but I couldn't use it much. Tube feedings are incredibly rich, some brands with 450 calories in six ounces, so if you aren't accustomed to them, a few spoonfuls can bring on crippling nausea. My diet then consisted mainly of pureed beef, chicken, pork, or seafood, mixed with vegetables, couscous, and sauce. The result was reasonably tasty food with enough texture to remain appetizing but not so much that it required chewing, and enough sauce to make it easy to swallow but not so much that it would be runny and thus easy to aspirate.

In packing for the New York road trip, we needed a lot of gear: my snazzy electric wheelchair, my office chair in which I sit every day, my shower chair, a few days' worth of clothing, an I.V. drip pole to hang tube feedings, three kinds of pre-made meals which had to be kept cool, a mattress overlay which prevents bedsores, a medical supplies kit, and my computer. There was so much we needed two vehicles, my converted minivan and an SUV.

On the road, without strong neck muscles I cannot hold my head still, so every bump, pothole, turn, or deceleration makes my head feel as stable as a melon mounted on a soda straw. Five minutes into the trip we realized we had left the wheelchair charger at home, an easy fix, but that evening in the rolling hills of western Pennsylvania, we discovered that we had also forgotten my tube feeding syringes, which I needed to get proper amounts of fluid in my system. We drove around in rural Pennsylvania visiting a few all-night Walgreen's before we found a suitable replacement.

When we finally reached Manhattan, Volvo put us up at the W hotel in Times Square, a nice place but a bit too chic for my simpler Midwestern taste. Our first official function was a luncheon for the nine finalists, their spouses, and the judges. I met Hank Aaron, Sally Ride, and Eunice Kennedy Shriver. Senator Bill Bradley and Sir Richard Branson milled about among the other finalists.

I felt very proud listening to the CEO of Volvo, Anne Belec, describe Extra Hands. At that point we had operations running in seven cities: Boise, Boston, Dallas-Ft.Worth, Los Angeles, Orange County, the San Francisco Bay area, and St. Louis. Each area had fifty to sixty students guided by ten to fifteen mentors, serving fifteen to twenty ALS families. To run these operations we had a team of seven Program Managers, one in each city, who recruit, train, deploy, and monitor all program participants. At the St. Louis headquarters worked an administrator, an office manager, the CEO, and myself. We were on a pace then to produce about 40,000 volunteer hours annually, with a budget of about $450,000. That works out to about $11.00 per volunteer hour, compared to the national average of about $18.00.

I felt fulfilled listening to the description of the charity I had founded and built with my own two paralyzed hands, so to speak. When she finished describing Extra Hands she called my name and I drove my wheelchair up to the lectern. As she handed me a trophy – a very large safety pin in the shape of the Volvo SUV sticking out of a Lucite base with my name engraved on it – a photographer snapped a bunch of photos just like on the red carpet at the Oscars.

That evening, we drove down to the Times Square Studio for the award ceremony. As we drove across 43rd Street to the studio entrance, I could see an enormous picture of myself on the Times Square Trinitron. There I was, larger-than-life, eyes wide open, as if staring down anyone who might try to stop me. "Jack Orchard, hero," read the tag line. My search for a purposeful conclusion to my life had produced exciting results. I thought about the people across the country whom I'll never know, hundreds of them then, and thousands now, whose lives are better because of what they put in to Extra Hands. That's the secret of why

Extra Hands is so compelling – it's a bank of mutual beneficence; the more you put in, the more you and other contributors get out.

I also felt embarrassed because I wasn't the one who had contributed the most challenging gift to Extra Hands. That honor belongs to the many volunteers who opened themselves to friendships with people certain to die in the near future. There have been more than a few who have suffered that painful loss and then asked to do it again. That is true selflessness, signing up when you know you'll get hurt even though it would be so much easier to spend those two hours each week watching reruns of Law & Order. Sure, I had raised a bunch of money around an exciting idea, and I had put in the hours to make it work, but I had no choice. I simply could not die with my mind at rest if I had not chosen the path I took.

Inside the studio, we were escorted to a waiting room where all the finalists and judges nibbled on finger food. I talked with Eunice Kennedy Shriver, who sounded so much like her brothers it was eerie. One of the members of the Extra Hands Board of Directors at the time is a cousin of Julie Chen, an anchor on the CBS Early Show, and he had pitched to her the idea of doing a story about me. They interviewed me that evening in the waiting room, filmed the award ceremony, and then interviewed Eve and me in St. Louis the following month. The footage was used to produce a segment they run on the Early Show each month called 'American Hero.' It aired a month later and generated a lot of buzz about Extra Hands.

The award ceremony itself was entertaining. The audience included all the finalists and spouses, numerous celebrities, all the top management of Volvo, and dozens of reporters and photographers. The event had been timed to coincide with a major automobile show held at the Jacob Javits Convention Center, which draws the media from all over the world, and anyone with press credentials was invited to the award ceremony. Jim Belushi emceed the event, cracking jokes and announcing the various speakers. As flash bulbs popped like fireworks, the judges read descriptions of each of the finalists.

I thought then about another of my heroes, Sir Ernest Shackleton. He set out on an expedition to cross Antarctica in 1914, and when it failed, he turned his attention to saving his crew of twenty-seven men, a feat requiring incredible endurance and personal fortitude. I laughed to myself, remembering Shackleton's dry wit, as evidenced in the ad he placed in a newspaper looking for men for the expedition.

"Men wanted for hazardous journey. Small wages, bitter cold. Long months of complete darkness, constant danger, safe return doubtful. Honor and recognition in case of success."

My journey, from the first strange feeling in my hand to the Times Square Trinitron, had certainly been hazardous at times, and I had spent many long, dark months in emotional oblivion. And there I was, being honored for my "success." Was my safe return doubtful? Terminal illness is, by definition, a one-way trip.

Yet still I took some grim satisfaction then that my illness, which had pushed me to build something so meaningful to me, might also have drawn a new kind of map for others who find themselves lost in similarly harsh territory.

After the award ceremony, I stared out the windows of the second floor with Eve, watching the big Trinitron scroll through the nine finalists. We didn't talk much. In a way, I felt that we had regressed to the working relationship we never had in Moscow, familiar but distant. As the Trinitron scrolled I asked her to get a nice shot of my photograph when it came up so we could post it on the Extra Hands website. The floor thudded with the backbeat of the music from the Black Crowes' private concert, to which we were invited, on the floor below. By then I felt drained, malnourished from not being able to stomach the rich tube feedings or pureed meals we had brought. My voice was barely audible, and I didn't want to attend a loud concert where no one could understand me if I needed something. I went back to the hotel and went to sleep.

Back in St. Louis, we returned to our everyday routines. Eve had stopped working on Extra Hands over a year earlier. She spent her days gardening, going to yoga, studying Hinduism, and learning Sanskrit. We fought often, and grated on each other as we crossed paths each day. In one especially confrontational moment she told me about an ALS patient she had heard about who was on a tracheal ventilator for so long that he lost all ability to communicate. The man stayed that way for three years, a prisoner in his own body, unable to move even his eyes. His wife was emotionally devastated by the torment of knowing that the man she married was still in there, fully cognizant of his condition but unable to beg her to let him go.

And then Eve said, "If you choose to go on a trach I probably wouldn't stay with you."

I didn't know how to reply. I was stunned, speechless, deeply hurt, and absolutely furious. I felt that she was asking me to choose between her and a longer life. Not long after, I called a divorce attorney.

As part of our divorce, Eve took our dog, Ike, with her. We didn't discuss it. I figured he would likely outlive me, so it seemed the right thing to do to let him spend the rest of his dog days with at least one of the people who had raised him. But it stung. It still stings. I miss him every day. He had been such a powerful relief from grief for me in San Francisco, and I had grown accustomed to his routines.

He began each morning with the wake-up announcement in which he would approach me silently as I lay in bed. Then he would place his head on the bed directly in front of my face, and sigh heavily through his nose to blow on my face until I awoke. I'd open my eyes and look at him, and he'd respond by giving me a hello-lick and wagging his tail excitedly. Then he'd fetch my helper to begin my morning routine. Once I was safely on the toilet, and my helper would leave to give me a shred of privacy, Ike would stand guard at the bathroom door. He had noticed that when I was finished I would call for help, but as my voice got softer I had to put in a lot of effort to make myself audible. So Ike stepped up for me. The instant

I made any sound whatsoever, he would tear off into the kitchen barking to alert my helper that I was ready. I didn't teach him to be my voice. He recognized the patterns of my daily life and filled in when he sensed he had a role to play.

In mid-February 2005, Kristen Williamson walked into my office. She is an amateur triathlete, and wanted to do a race in memory of a friend's father who had recently died with ALS. He had been in the Extra Hands program. Kristen came to my office with a friend, Ella Wood, to learn about how to raise donations for Extra Hands based on their participation in the St. Louis Marathon in early April. Extra Hands had sponsored other athletes before. We even had tools to do what they wanted available on our website.

Kristen has long black hair; she's tall, tanned, in great shape, and has a ready smile and dark, sparkling eyes. But it wasn't how she looked that struck me. As she and Ella spoke about what they wanted to do, I remember thinking how genuine she seemed. The more Kristen spoke that day in my office, the more I realized that all she wanted to do was to participate in a race, and she figured someone might as well benefit from it. Her friend's father had recently died, and she had heard about Extra Hands, so here she was.

Instead of explaining the webtools available on our site, which was all they really needed, I turned the conversation around to an idea I had been thinking about for some time already.

"What would it take," I asked, "to make it possible for anyone, not just in St. Louis, but anywhere, to participate in an athletic event and raise money for Extra Hands like you two?" I knew enough by then to understand how important it was to set things up correctly for a campaign to be successful. People want to make a difference, but often they need to be motivated in very specific, measurable ways.

"Free stuff," said Kristen. "As athletes raise money for Extra Hands you could give them training gear like racing jerseys, or fleece jackets...."

"From corporate sponsors," said Ella. "You could ask companies to donate some stuff, and give discounts to sponsored athletes..."

"You could also put your logo on everything," added Kristen, "so sponsored athletes can feel like they're connected to a team."

I liked their enthusiasm. They had the same infectious energy as many of the Extra Hands student volunteers. "Would you two be interested in taking the lead on this?" I asked.

They smiled and looked at each other. "Sure!" said Kristen. "When are you thinking about doing this?"

"Yesterday," I said.

That really got them excited. Kristen explained that she worked from home as an analyst with Procter & Gamble, so she had very flexible hours, and she had plenty of friends in the St. Louis Triathlon Club who might also be interested. Ella worked at an accounting firm so she couldn't be quite as active before April 15th, but she was eager to get involved too. When they left my office I wondered if they thought I was crazy dumping a whole campaign in their laps, but Kristen emailed me a few hours later with an outline for a national plan of action and the steps she had already taken. Crazy or not, it was the right choice. Or maybe she was crazy too?

We traded e-mail messages back and forth as she methodically worked through her plan. After a few weeks, we began to drift off of work topics. I asked how she had gotten into triathlons originally. She explained how Procter & Gamble had moved her to Iowa right out of college, and because she didn't know anyone there she started working out. During the long hours biking past cornfields she said she found a serene beauty in them. I had already been impressed by her work style, and that comment made me interested in finding out more about her.

The next time I saw her was in April at the St. Louis Marathon. I had forgotten what she looked like – I'm terrible remembering faces – but she found me wandering in my wheelchair with my helper. She introduced me to a group of her friends from Des Moines who had run the marathon on behalf of Extra Hands, and we all stood around the finish line chatting about the event. I was excited because it was the first official event for the campaign we now call the Extra Hands Athletic Challenge – we offer athletes of all types and abilities across the nation an online training regimen, free jerseys and embroidered warm-up gear, and a personal website to help publicize their events to friends and family.

Then a few weeks later she came to my office to drop off some racing jerseys we had ordered as part of the free giveaways. Although I still had a wisp of my voice left, it took all my energy to speak, so she sat close to be able to read from my computer as I typed what I wanted to say. After chatting for a few minutes, I felt energized and wanted to spend more time with her. "Do you like hot chocolate?" I typed.

"Uhm, yes..." She gave me a kind of funny look.

"Wanna go get the best hot chocolate in town?" I asked.

"Well...I have an hour to kill," she said. "Why not? Sure."

It was a beautiful spring day, sunny and seventy degrees. We drove to my favorite coffee shop and sat outside at a sidewalk table. During the hour we spent together – I don't remember what we talked about – there was a brief moment when she caught me staring at her. It suddenly hit me; she's smart, she's talented, she's funny, and...wow! – she's beautiful! I had caught her staring at me too.

We started spending time together, and trading silly gifts. At one point she said how she wished her job was more fulfilling emotionally. "After all," she said, "it's not like anyone's life is better because of Charmin toilet paper."

"Don't be so sure about that," I replied. I told her about a trip I had once taken to Arkhangelsk, a Russian city way up above the Arctic Circle on the White Sea, to visit a large paper mill. I got food poisoning there, and had to leave one of my meetings urgently to visit the bathroom. It was unspeakably filthy, well beyond your worst nightmare, but I had no choice. So I breathed through my mouth only, and tried bending over the toilet without sitting on it. It worked well enough. When I finished I looked up for the toilet paper, but there was none. I couldn't believe it. In the entire world, is there no better place to find a roll of toilet paper than at a goddamned paper mill?! Instead, some industrious devotee of recycling had torn the morning newspaper into strips. I cleaned up as well as I could and returned to my meeting.

"Nobody, man or woman, knows toilet terror the way I knew it then," I explained to Kristen. "And I would have given my left arm for a roll of Charmin." A few days later I got a package at work – a roll of Charmin. A short time later an article about Extra Hands appeared in the St. Louis Post-Dispatch. Kristen emailed me, asking if she could have my autograph. After losing the use of my hands, I had taken a copy of my signature to a print shop, and had them make a rubber stamp of it. So I replied that Kristen could have several, then had my helper stamp each sheet on the Charmin roll, wrap it like a birthday present, and deliver it.

I was drawn to Kristen's fiery, never-in-neutral personality. She doesn't do anything halfway no matter how important or trivial. She loved riding her racing bike, so she became a triathlete, competing in triathlons and marathons across the country. To do so required overcoming real fears. Just a week after buying her bike she was out training when she approached an intersection. In the direction she was riding there was no stop sign, but crossing traffic was supposed to stop and yield. As Kristen entered the intersection, a woman driving on the crossing road to her left rolled through the stop. It happened so fast Kristen had no time to get out of her way. The car slammed into her so hard it left an impression of its grill on her leg for weeks after the accident. But that wasn't the worst of it. The collision threw her from the bike. She landed on her head so hard her bike helmet cracked in two, and then her mouth hit the pavement. The impact smashed out her four upper front teeth. She got up, dusted herself off, and tried dialing 911 on her cell-phone but couldn't speak intelligibly without her teeth. The woman who hit her had gotten out of her car, and was sitting on the sidewalk crying hysterically. With blood pouring down her chin and jersey, Kristen shoved the phone in the woman's hand and made her ask for help. Afterward, Kristen needed so much re-constructive work on her teeth and gums that she vis-ited a dentist every week for months. The dentist's of-fice staff got to know her so well they invited her to their Christmas party.

I was lucky Kristen didn't feel neutral about me. Was it the strength of her emotions that enabled her to look past my disability to see me for the man I am instead of the quadriplegic? Soon it was apparent, to both of us, that our closeness was not exactly pla-tonic. "What could you possibly get out of a relation-ship with me," I asked her, "that you can't get from a healthy guy? I'm the definition of high-maintenance."

Kristen didn't hesitate in her answer. "I want someone who inspires me," she said. "And you're the most inspiring person I know." She didn't have to en-ter a relationship with me. When my time comes, whatever pain she will feel will have been magnified by our intimacy. But her choice shows that she shares a crucially important part of my worldview – that we live for today. It's not that I don't want to die, but that I want to live, and Kristen's choice is life-affirming.

Although I take a lot of pills each day, Viagra isn't one of them. ALS involves the loss of all voluntary muscle control – arms, legs, hands, and so on – but as any sixteen-year old boy can tell you, some changes in the male anatomy are not exactly voluntary. To commemorate our emerging love affair, I took her to my favorite building in St. Louis for a photograph of the two of us beneath the large sign bearing the name of the company located there. It's the headquarters of the St. Louis Steel Erection Company.

Kristen's drive also pushed me to confront the issues I let overtake my marriage to Eve. The morning after one of the first times she stayed overnight with me, she grabbed a pair of socks and started putting them on me. She had already noticed that the first thing my helper does in the morning is put on my socks, shoes, and braces, so I can stand and transfer to my shower wheelchair.

"Please don't do that," I said firmly. "Let my helper put them on."

"What, do you think I need training to put on your socks?" she teased. With Eve, caregiving started as an expression of her love for me, but turned into a prison for her. Now, Kristen wanted to show her feelings for me in the same way, and even though it was just a simple pair of socks, I could hear the grind of metal on metal as the prison door began to move.

"You have to understand," I said. "I lost my wife like this."

"Well, I'm not your wife," she said with a smirk. "And I want to put your socks on. So if you don't like that, you just try and stop me."

I suppose I deserved that. But Kristen has made me stronger for it. I am different in the way I ask for and accept help from her than I was with Eve. I rarely let her get in a situation where she's the only one around to help me, and I'm careful to give her the freedom to let my helper step in before she gets over-whelmed. Finding the equilibrium is quite a challenge. If my helpers are in the next room twenty-four hours a day, we have no real privacy. Yet without them the prison door slides smoothly on a greased track. Somewhere in between the extremes lies a delicate so-lution that changes ever so slightly each day. But the constant search for it removes the subtext in our dis-cussions about caregiving. It's not about dignity, just affection.

It helps that Kristen is naturally a considerate, caring person, someone who takes action instinctively. Once, she noticed that my Dad has difficulty standing from the low couch in my study where we watch base-ball games together. The next evening, the instant the game was over she jumped up from her seat and rushed over to help him up. In the winter she often walked him to his car to make sure he didn't slip on any snow or ice. And when one of my helpers got hit by a car while biking home, she bought him a helmet.

It also helps that Kristen doesn't shrink before the challenges I deal with every day. She figures out solutions to whatever gets in my or our way and just plows ahead. She jokes about how her solution to everything is to slap on some Neosporin and an ace bandage, although in fact she's pretty creative. Her solution for pressure sores, an unfortunate peril for anyone with a movement disability, is a great example. I usually sleep on my right side but I don't move much at all during the night, so I developed a pressure sore on my right ear. Pressure sores can get infected easily, they can be extremely painful, and they can take months to heal. We tried positioning me on my left side, but that hip would ache so badly I just couldn't get to sleep.

Kristen bought some foam padding, the kind often used to soften the surface of a firm mattress, and cut a doughnut-shaped cushion out of it. Each night we get me positioned on my right side and then she places the "ear pillow" under my head with my ear in the hole in the middle. The result is that my ear remains suspended off the surface of the pillow, while the weight of my head gets distributed across more than a square foot of foam cushion. It's a $0.95 solution, and it works perfectly.

Just as Ike had been my faithful companion in the dark days of my descent toward a diagnosis, I figured I could benefit from another furry friend. Kristen wanted a dog too, especially as a running companion, so she took charge of the search, going online to look through dogs at nearby shelters. Eventually, she found a seven-week old, male, black lab mix puppy at a shelter in Rolla, Missouri, about a 90-minute drive away.

He had been found with several brothers and sisters some weeks earlier with no mother in sight. But the shelter couldn't keep them; they were scheduled to be euthanized the next morning. So Kristen raced out to Rolla and picked the runt of the litter.

She walked in my front door carrying his little four-pound body in one hand. He stank of urine from the foul pen where he and many other strays lived at the overcrowded shelter. But after his first bath, with his tiny tail wagging incessantly, he excitedly checked out his new home, slipping often on the hardwood floor and peeing everywhere as if he'd had a giant cup of coffee. "What should we name him?" Kristen asked. His clumsiness and lack of manners gave me an idea about that. When I was in graduate school at Stanford, a classmate there had a funny habit of teasing his friends for their maladroit moments with the opposite sex or any other indelicate maneuver by calling us "Teds." I don't know the origin of the joke but it caught on among the group of guys with whom I was close there. One night near graduation day, my six housemates and I held a party at the rental house where we lived. I got very drunk, and after passing out on my bed they wrote "I'm a Ted" all over me – forehead, arms, legs – in permanent marker. It took almost a week of scrubbing to get it off, but I deserved it, believe me. So when Kristen asked me what we should name our dog, I had just the right name.

Ted is extraordinarily tedly after all. He has webbed feet reflecting the Labrador retriever in his DNA, but he's terrified of water. Kristen and I like to hang out by my parents' pool and try to teach him to swim, but he even runs away when she turns on a hose to water the wildflowers we're growing in the back of my home. She could line the pool with fresh-cooked bacon, and he still won't go near it. He is such a Ted, and he has no idea how lucky he is to have his mama's love.

Heroes are selfless and courageous, people who put their hearts at risk. Kristen fell in love with a dying man, so despite being in perfect health she confronts mortality every day by my side. I can be direct and honest with her. Neither of us sugarcoats reality. We've talked about where my illness leads, and what her life will be like after I'm gone. She half-jokes when she says, "After my nervous breakdown after you're gone..." But rather than dwell on the harshness of the future, we live in the present, purposefully trying to squeeze the most out of each day together. One of the wonderful results is that I have never been so immersed in affection and tenderness as I am now. It's an act of heroism to open yourself to another person. To allow yourself to be seen for who you really are, and to see the other for who he is requires true courage. To accept another person's mortality is to accept your own. I am not a hero, but I know one.

Chapter Ten

Flashes Across the Darkness

♦♦♦♦♦♦♦

Summers in St. Louis are hot and steamy. The mercury often climbs into the 90s, and the humidity makes it feel even higher. I remember, from my childhood, the long, sticky days with my shirt plastered to my skin and the air so wet and heavy I could almost wade through it. Locusts buzz in the trees, calling each other. Their song pulsates, rising and falling in unison. I used to play golf in this sort of swelter, happy to venture out when I knew retirees would stay in and leave the course to me. Afterward I'd guzzle sweet tea in the parking lot while airing out my car. It was an orange 1976 Fiat, a box on wheels I inherited when Connie went away to college, and its vinyl seats and black plastic steering wheel could scald if I jumped in too quickly. St. Louis is a good place to grow up, and I suppose it's as good a place as any in which to die.

I am dying. I can't talk, eat, or walk. I can't change the TV channel, or guzzle sweet tea. I need someone to put on my socks, brush my hair off my ears, and scratch my nose when it tickles. I spend every day in my study sitting in an office chair. When I need something I use my eyes to type out messages on a fancy, eye-tracking computer I bought when my last useful finger, the one needed to click a mouse, started to fade out.

Yet my life has never felt fuller. Extra Hands, which continues to grow, keeps me connected to many people around the country, some brave and inspiring, some desperate and despondent, but all breaking out of the isolation that ALS brings. I receive email from them, dozens of messages each day, and I answer them as sincerely as I can. Sometimes I know exactly what to say; either I've felt something they're going through or I've solved a similar problem in my own battle with ALS. Sometimes I'm stumped.

I get out of the house most weekends to see a movie with friends or attend family dinners at my parents' home where my nieces and nephews bounce around the dinner table like pinballs. The eldest, Connie's son Drew who is eleven years old, has become an inquisitive, thoughtful adolescent. When he was a toddler I used to play bucking bronco with him; he'd try to stay on my back as I wiggled and shook on all fours. But his sister, Claire, and Harry's children, Ethan, Lily, and Poppy, all came along too late for me to play with them. That has been one of the greater disappointments of my condition, that I couldn't develop much of a relationship with them. Someday Drew may remember the fun we had together but to the others I'll likely be just a hazy image in a wheelchair.

My Dad comes over often to watch baseball games with me. My Mom occasionally comes with him, and regularly exercises her impressive ability to share a little gossip precisely during the most crucial moments of the game. Connie and Harry visit when they can get away from their parental duties, and Jay likes to spend his days off from work taking care of the yard around my home.

Kristen and I make the most of every day. She kisses the bald spot on my head before going to work, and usually comes home at lunch to share an hour with me and Ted. After work, at dusk, we like to turn off all the lights in the house and sit on the deck watching fireflies as they light up and dance in the back yard, like fairies. They glide quietly in the steamy, humid weather. But when the heat breaks in a tremendous Midwestern thunderstorm, and the air turns green from the low pressure and the static electricity, their dance accelerates. The males dart and swoop through the air, luminescent, signaling to the females, who in turn flash back. Although the firefly waltz may seem random and wild, there is, nevertheless, a choreography to it. It ranks among the most beautiful things I've ever seen.

If we are lucky, our lives too are luminescent, and filled with more soaring highs than plunging lows. Through our experiences and encounters we gain insight into ourselves, into the barely recognizable patterns of our existence that make us all unique but similar to each other, and interconnected. My pattern has followed a grand arc – from my childhood grounded in reason, to Greece where I began to dig deeper for my own answers, to Moscow where I soared with the new economy and fell in love, to San Francisco where my light flickered. And then there was the terrible darkness when I came to terms with my diagnosis, my limitations, and my mortality. But my luminescence returned, brighter than before, when I founded Extra Hands for ALS, and I have continued to shine as it has thrived and prospered, all of its participants flashing signals to one another – I'm here. I'm scared. You are not alone. We can find meaning together by bringing out the best in one another. No matter what our muscles can do, we all have the same ability to improve our lot. Always, always, each of us is a flash across the darkness.

Flashing lights play an unusually large role in my daily life. The computer which tracks my eye movements flashes when my gaze dwells on a letter for a quarter-second. My flashing signals create words, sentences, paragraphs – this book of my dying, which is also a book of my life. When I'm alone in my study, as I am most days, I do what I enjoy most of all; I read, I think, I answer e-mails from family, friends, teammates, and strangers. After many years spent exploring the world, trying new things, and challenging myself to press further and climb higher, I have found serenity in the relative monotony and silence of my workaday routines. Although the quiet repetition of my days might drive a fully functional person insane with boredom, I love every minute of it because I can still do it unaided. When I quit for the night to go to bed, I can't wait to get up the next morning and do it again.

In my dreams I am almost always fully functional. My voice is strong. I run up steps, ski down slopes, hold a cup steady to my lips. It's as if my subconscious doesn't want to let go of my old self, so in the solitude of a midnight reverie it plays out who I used to be. I once read an article about the theory that dreams are a way for our minds to conjure up alternative realities, so if we face them in real life we will be better prepared to handle them. At least, so said an evolutionary biologist who wanted to conclude there is a survival benefit to be gained through our dreams. Separately, I read another article about a class in which one can learn to become aware that one is dreaming without waking up, and then manipulate the events that occur in the dream. I was fascinated, and some weeks after reading about it, I dreamed I was walking and chatting with friends. Although I wasn't manipulating the action of the dream, it was very clear that the event in it was of my own design. I had dreamed what I wanted to be doing, and at night, with the aid of my subconscious I did it.

Sleep, for nineteenth-century poets like John Keats, who died at the age of twenty-six from tuberculosis, was often a metaphor for death, and correspondingly, the awakening the next morning symbolized the emergence into the afterlife. It's tempting to believe in life after death. We fear the finality of death, so humans have been concocting ideas about what comes next as long as we have pondered our origins.

We also wonder about our last moments. Will I be in pain? Will I be alone? Will I have left some important task unfinished? How can you feel ready for your death with so much mystery surrounding it? Not long ago I realized that the frustrating but ultimately insignificant details of my daily life as a quadriplegic would be offset by an extraordinary gift I have received – I know how and when I will die. I know what it will feel like because I've done a trial run.

Last year I got in a fight with pneumonia, and got clobbered. While in the pulmonary intensive care unit trying to fight off the infection in my lungs, one of them collapsed. Suddenly I couldn't breathe at all, even wearing a ventilator over my mouth and nose. Nurses and doctors darted into my room in response to various alarms screaming through the quiet nighttime ward. As the oxygen content of my blood descended second by second, I writhed in bed suffocating.

"Jack, we're going to give you something to help you relax," I remember my doctor said. And then...nothing.

The next thing I remember was his cheerful voice greeting me as morning sunshine poured in through the window. A ventilator quietly pushed air into my lungs through a new tube inserted in my neck. I thought they had knocked me out, fixed my collapsed lung, and performed a tracheostomy all in one extended crisis. But I later learned I had been awake and communicative for five days with a ventilation tube shoved in my mouth and down into my windpipe while I waited for my scheduled surgery. They had given me a drug to prevent me from remembering those uncomfortable days.

Death will be like that, I think. A hospice nurse will give me a dose of morphine to put me to sleep and then steadily dial down my ventilator until my heart stops. And I will experience...nothing. The mysteries that you feel about your own death no longer plague me because I'll choose the moment, I'll surround myself with family, and I'll tell them one last time that I love them.

      The forest green walls of my study are covered with dozens of pictures of me with family and friends. Here I am with Harry and Dad at Jackson Hole, Wyoming in the summer of 1979. We're holding up the fish we caught at Jackson Lake. There I am laughing with my friend, Charlie Ryan, at an après-ski bar in Avoriaz, Switzerland in 1992. We're about to drain our beers and stagger back to our chalet. On the opposite wall I have a picture of my high school football teammates and I relaxing in Andy Katzman's hot tub in 1984. Neither snow nor rain nor heat nor gloom of night stayed the "Hot Tub Club" from meeting every Sunday evening. Next to it is a picture of my nephew, Drew, and I playing in a pile of leaves at my parents' home after the fall raking in 1997. He has leaves stuck all over his little yellow fleece pullover, and he's laughing his infectious laugh.

      My family and friends like to come over and look at the photos, and occasionally they'll add to my collection, like the one of my dad lying naked on the beach at St. Barth's in 1993. That's a recent addition. If it's not true that when you die, your life flashes before you, this room will be an excellent substitute. When my time comes I would like to be surrounded, one way or another, by the people who have meant so much to me, who have shaped my life, the people to whom I am connected, to whom I am responsible, and on whom I rely.

But there is so much left to do, so for now, back to work…

Visit the Extra Hands for ALS website!

www.extrahands.org

Please consider a donation today. Extra Hands for ALS is a 501(c)3 public charity. All donations are tax-exempt to the extent permitted by law. You can send this form to the address below or donate via the Extra Hands website.

Thank you! We are grateful for your support!

Name on card _____

Address   _____

City, State, Zip _____

_____ Visit   Tel._____

_____ Master   Email _____

_____ Check   Acct. # _____

_____ Bill me   Exp. Date_____

Our address:
Extra Hands for ALS
36 Four Seasons Center, Suite 293
St. Louis, MO 63017